How to Remember Everything in the Doctrine and Covenants and Church History

by David R. Larsen

CFI
Springville, Utah

ISBN: 978-1-59955-239-2

Published by CFI, an imprint of Cedar Fort, Inc., 2373 W. 700 S., Springville, UT 84663
Distributed by Cedar Fort, Inc., www.cedarfort.com

Cover design by Angela Olsen
Cover design © 2008 by Lyle Mortimer
Edited and typeset by Jessica Stout

Printed in the United States of America

10 9 8 7 6 5 4 3 2 1

Printed on acid-free paper

How to Remember Everything in the Doctrine and Covenants and Church History

ALSO BY DAVID R. LARSEN

How to Remember Everything in the Old Testament

How to Remember Everything in the New Testament and General Conference

How to Remember Everything in the Book of Mormon

CONTENTS

ACKNOWLEDGMENTS

I would like to acknowledge my pioneer ancestors and their contributions to Church history: Nahum Curtis, who lost most of his worldly goods to mobs in Missouri, and later his life in Nauvoo as he sought to follow a modern prophet; his son Lyman Curtis, one of Parley P. Pratt's advanced party scouts, and among the first three Latter-day Saints to stay overnight in the Salt Lake Valley near City Creek on July 22, 1847, so Brigham Young and the others would know where to go when they entered the Valley on the July 24; Bishop Alonzo Raleigh, a descendant of Sir Walter Raleigh, a statesman and bishop to Brother Brigham; Jonathan Campbell Jr., a member of the Mormon Battalion, and his wife

Charity who died crossing the plains; Jens Larsen Jorgensen and Bertha Sophia Anderson who heeded the call of the prophet to leave their homeland in Helsingor, Denmark, and gather in the West, and to their son, Adam, who lost much of his hearing as a young boy when persecutors rolled him down a hill in a barrel; and the Rose, Peel, Chadwick, Burton, Hirschi, and other pioneer families who became my ancestors.

Without their faith and diligence this book may never have been written.

And especially my wife, Maureen, who found all of these and helped them to all come alive again for me through her diligent study of Church history. She also reviewed the various manuscripts for this book. I hope one day with practice I will be as diligent a learner and able to remember half as much as she does.

I also want to acknowledge the efforts of Jessica Best, who worked beyond the call of duty to prepare this for press.

INTRODUCTION

Recently, I was talking with a member of the Church who told me that although he has become much better organized in recent years, with the aid of modern technology he is finding that his short-term memory is declining—and he's not yet forty years of age.

How could that be? And what are the implications? In chapters 3 and 6 I discuss some factors that contribute to a decline in memory, not the least of which is a lack of exercise (actually both mental and physical). The brain needs exercise. Although the brain comprises more fats than muscle, like a muscle it is very much a use-it-or-lose-it organ. In the modern world with so many memory aids at our disposal, there is a real danger of Latter-day Saints losing their ability to remember specific counsel from the Lord.

In short, the implications are huge. Many do not realize the quality of our decisions, and therefore the outcomes in our lives, are based primarily on two things: 1) what we have experienced and the lessons learned from that experience, and 2) what we can remember of what we learned. We nearly always make judgments and choices based on what we are thinking at the time, which is fully dependent upon what we can remember. If in a moment of crisis we can recall relevant guidance from the Lord, our choices and counsel to our children are likely to be much wiser and the outcomes more rewarding than when they result from instinct, classical conditioning, TV programming, or peer modeling.

Not only is this pertinent to our mortal period of probation, but Joseph Smith suggested it may be relevant to the quality of our eternal life as well. D&C 130:19 says, "If a person gains more knowledge and intelligence in this life *through his diligence and obedience* than another, he will have so much the advantage in the world to come" (emphasis added). But note that this advantage requires diligence on our part. We can't just sit in church and expect the sermons to stick as they float through our ears like echoes in an empty drum. Nor does retinal exposure equate to remembering as we read the scriptures. This will likely not enable us to recall all we need to know in eternity. What many people may not fully appreciate is that learning and gaining knowledge require more active processes. They require thinking and connecting the thoughts in our brain. The quality of that thinking is dependent in large measure on the extent of our memory. So as we are more diligent in our studies, as we make an effort to remember more, we become more inclined to obedience and related benefits.

I hope, therefore, that you, the reader, will find in this book practical tools and techniques which when practiced and applied will enable you to retain much more of the wisdom imparted by the Lord in this marvelous modern scripture and in Church history.

1

THAT WE MIGHT ALWAYS REMEMBER

"Remember, remember . . ."
—D&C 3:3

One of the most important and oft repeated admonitions in all of ancient scripture is the commandment to "remember." It is repeated more than 210 times in the Bible and more than 75 times in the Book of Mormon. Apparently the Lord saw the Latter-day Saints as being in as much need of this admonition as any other generation. Although the Doctrine and Covenants is only about half as large as the Book of Mormon, it has nearly two-thirds as many reminders to remember or not forget.

Of the forty-five references to remembering in the Doctrine

and Covenants, five of these are petitions asking God to remember the Saints, primarily in sections 109 and 121.

In two other sections the Lord notes specific individuals who will be remembered (see D&C 108:4 and 124:78). Being remembered is considered to be one of the highest honors in eternity, whereas one of the greatest curses, as noted in the Old Testament, is to be forgotten. In fact, being forgotten is still probably one of the worst things that could happen to a person, either a child or a senior, in society today.

Thirty-six occurrences of *remember* are admonitions or encouragements to members. These admonitions occur in twenty-four of the 138 sections, more than one out of every six sections. This admonition was given more often than almost any other admonition in the Doctrine and Covenants, even the admonition to pray (twenty-three times), but less than the admonition to repent (forty-two times). Therefore, we might say that in the Doctrine and Covenants, the Lord is admonishing His people more than anything else to repent and to remember Him, His counsel, their covenants, and to pray often.

Two references are in section 20: the sacrament prayers. The Lord tries to make sure that we "get it" by commanding us every week to renew our covenant to remember Him, "that [we] may always have his Spirit to be with [us]" (v. 77).

Why is remembering so important? Perhaps the most compelling reason is because most of our emotions and actions are based on what we can remember. It's unlikely we will follow the counsel of the Lord if we can't remember what He told us to do.

What Are We to Remember?

The scriptures in the Doctrine and Covenants on remembering are generally more specific and insightful than similar admonitions in the other scriptures. So it will be valuable to review what things the Lord specifically has directed His people to remember in latter-day Church history. To make this more relevant and memorable to you, follow Nephi's counsel to liken these verses to yourself. What would be the implications if the Lord made these statements directly to you?

To emphasize this topic, in section 3 the Lord (as did Mosiah and Alma) starts with the double admonition, "Remember, remember," and then notes, "it is not the work of God that is frustrated, but the work of men" (v. 3). He admonishes, "**Remember** also the promises which were made to you, if you did not transgress them [the commandments]" (v. 5). "But **remember,** God is merciful; therefore, repent of that which thou hast done which is contrary to the commandment which I gave you" (v. 10).

In D&C 4:6 those who serve God are directed to "**Remember** faith, virtue, knowledge, temperance, patience, brotherly kindness, godliness, charity, humility, diligence."

D&C 6:10 says, "Behold thou hast a gift, and blessed art thou because of thy gift. **Remember** it is sacred and cometh from above."

The Lord admonishes Oliver Cowdery, in D&C 8:5 and 10, to "**Remember** these words, and keep my commandments. **Remember**, this [the spirit of revelation] is your gift. . . . **Remember** that without faith you can do nothing; therefore ask in faith. Trifle not with these things; do not ask for that which you ought not."

D&C 10:70 says, "And now, **remember** the words of him who is the life and light of the world your Redeemer, your Lord and your God. Amen."

D&C 18:10: "**Remember** the worth of souls is great in the sight of God."

D&C 20:77 and 79 are the sacrament prayers:

> O God, the Eternal Father, we ask thee in the name of thy Son, Jesus Christ, to bless and sanctify this bread to the souls of all those who partake of it, that they may eat in remembrance of the body of thy Son, and witness unto thee, O God, the Eternal Father, that they are willing to take upon them the name of thy Son, and always **remember** him and keep his commandments which he has given them; that they may always have his Spirit to be with them. Amen. . . .

> O God, the Eternal Father, we ask thee in the name of thy Son, Jesus Christ, to bless and sanctify this wine to the souls of all those who drink of it, that they may do it in remembrance of the blood of thy Son, which was shed for them; that they may witness unto thee, O God, the Eternal Father, that they do always **remember** him, that they may have his Spirit to be with them. Amen.

To six elders shortly before the first conference of the Church, the Lord said, "Behold, verily, verily, I say unto you, that at this time your sins are forgiven you, therefore ye receive these things; but **remember** to sin no more, lest perils shall come upon you. . . . But **remember** that all my judgments are not given unto men; and as the words have gone forth out of my mouth even so shall they be fulfilled" (D&C 29: 3, 30).

D&C 33:12 and 14: "Behold, verily, verily, I say unto you, this is my gospel; and **remember** that they shall have faith in me or they can in nowise be saved; . . . And ye shall **remember** the church articles and covenants to keep them."

D&C 42:30 and 79: "And behold, thou wilt **remember** the poor, and consecrate of thy properties for their support that which thou hast to impart unto them, with a covenant and a deed which cannot be broken. . . . And it shall come to pass, that if any persons among you shall kill they shall be delivered up and dealt with according to the laws of the land; for **remember** that he hath no forgiveness; and it shall be proved according to the laws of the land."

D&C 46:8 and 10: "Wherefore, beware lest ye are deceived; and that ye may not be deceived seek ye earnestly the best gifts, **always remembering** for what they are given; . . . And again, verily I say unto you, I would that ye should **always remember**, and **always** retain in your minds what those gifts are, that are given unto the church."

The emphasis of **always** seems significant here. Have you consistently retained in your mind (or your memory) what those gifts are, and for what they are given? Could you state them if asked?

D&C 52:40: "And **remember** in all things the poor and the

needy, the sick and the afflicted, for he that doeth not these things, the same is not my disciple."

D&C 58:5: "**Remember** this, which I tell you before, that you may lay it to heart, and receive that which is to follow."

Remembering what you've been told will prepare you to receive more intelligence.

D&C 59:12: "But **remember** that on this, the Lord's day, thou shalt offer thine oblations and thy sacraments unto the Most High, confessing thy sins unto thy brethren, and before the Lord."

D&C 63:64: "**Remember** that that which cometh from above is sacred, and must be spoken with care, and by constraint of the Spirit; and in this there is no condemnation, and ye receive the Spirit through prayer; wherefore, without this there remaineth condemnation."

D&C 68:30: "And the inhabitants of Zion also shall **remember** their labors inasmuch as they are appointed to labor, in all faithfulness; for the idler shall be had in remembrance before the Lord."

D&C 84:57: "And they shall remain under this condemnation until they repent and **remember** the new covenant, even the Book of Mormon and the former commandments which I have given them, not only to say, but to do according to that which I have written."

D&C 88:69: "**Remember** the great and last promise which I have made unto you; cast away your idle thoughts and your excess of laughter far from you."

D&C 89:18: "And all saints who **remember** to keep and do these sayings, walking in obedience to the commandments, shall receive health in their navel and marrow to their bones" (see chapter 6).

D&C 90:24: "Search diligently, pray always, and be believing, and all things shall work together for your good, if ye walk uprightly and **remember** the covenants wherewith ye have covenanted one with another."

D&C 108:4: "Wait patiently until the solemn assembly shall

be called of my servants, then you shall be **remembered** with the first of mine elders, and receive right by ordination with the rest of mine elders whom I have chosen."

D&C 117:16: "And again, verily I say unto you, let all my servants in the land of Kirtland **remember** the Lord their God, and mine house also, to keep and preserve it holy."

D&C 124:14: "But let him **remember** that his stewardship will I require at his hands."

D&C 128:6: "And further, I want you to **remember** that John the Revelator was contemplating this very subject in relation to the dead, when he declared, as you will find recorded in Revelation 20:12."

Additionally, to Oliver Cowdery the Lord noted there are certain things that are good to forget. We will discuss this further in the next chapter.

D&C 9:9: "But if it be not right you shall have no such feelings, but you shall have a stupor of thought that shall cause you to forget the thing which is wrong; therefore, you cannot write that which is sacred save it be given you from me."

Too often we forget the right and **remember** the wrong things. And so the Lord concludes with this ominous warning: "The Lord who shall suddenly come to his temple; the Lord who shall come down upon the world with a curse to judgment; yea, upon all the nations that forget God, and upon all the ungodly among you" (D&C 133:2).

Is that not relevant for us today with our current challenges in the world? In any event it is clear there are many things that the Lord feels are important, if not essential for us to **remember.** That is the rationale behind this book. I hope it will help you to remember all that is good and true and important for you in the Doctrine and Covenants and Church history.

2

TAKING THE HOLY SPIRIT AS OUR GUIDE

"For they that are wise . . . have taken the Holy Spirit as their guide."
—D&C 45:57

The restoration of the gospel brought a new spiritual awakening to the world. For centuries people had been taught that God no longer spoke with men and that revelation had ceased. But during the Restoration, people were anxious to hear the voice of the Lord and experience the gifts of the Spirit. They were ripe for receiving the gospel, which is why so many joined the Church in those early days.

The Lord directed the Saints to seek earnestly the "best gifts" of the Spirit (D&C 46:8), for not all of the spirits that were manifest at that time were of the Lord and not all of their gifts were of God.

Satan, seeing how the Saints were eager to receive spiritual gifts, was anxious to fill this void and answer the aspirations of those seeking enlightenment with counterfeit spiritual phenomena. Just as in our day, he and other false spirits were "abroad in the land"[1] and the Saints were not immune to false spirits' influences and deceptions. Indeed they, as we are, were likely prime targets for his evil influence.

Perhaps that is why when, after his death, Joseph Smith appeared to Brigham Young and when Brigham Young later appeared to Wilford Woodruff, their messages were essentially the same—to learn to discern the Spirit.

On February 23, 1847, Brigham Young recorded the following vision and message from the deceased Prophet Joseph Smith.

> Tell the people to be humble and faithful, and be sure to keep the Spirit of the Lord and it will lead them right. Be careful and not turn away the still small voice; it will teach them what to do and where to go; it will yield the fruits of the kingdom. Tell the [people] to keep their hearts open to conviction, so that when the Holy Ghost comes to them, their hearts will be ready to receive it. They can tell the Spirit of the Lord from all other spirits; it will whisper peace and joy to their souls; it will take malice, hatred, strife and all evil from their hearts; and their whole desire will be to do good, bring forth righteousness and build up the kingdom of God. Tell the [people] if they will follow the spirit of the Lord, they will go right.[2]

There is a similar quote from a visitation by Brigham Young to Wilford Woodruff in 1880 while Woodruff was president of the Church (Brigham Young died in 1877). During their visit Brigham Young said, "I want you to teach the people—and I want you to follow this counsel yourself—that they must labor and so live as to obtain the Holy Spirit, for without this you cannot build up the kingdom; without the Spirit of God you are in danger of walking in the dark, and in danger of failing to accomplish your calling as apostles and as Elders in the church and kingdom of God."[3]

Now, just as then, we must learn to discern, to learn how to receive or access the Spirit of the Lord in guiding us and our families through these counterfeits and perilous times. An essential part of discerning is gaining the gifts and guidance of the Spirit to help us learn and remember those things that would enable us to be wise and distinguish good from evil. It is imperative that we have this Holy influence to help avoid the deceptions of the adversary and successfully overcome our trials to fulfill our missions and the purposes of the Lord. We also need to learn and remember the scriptures most relevant for us in doing this.

There are two good companion volumes for this study of the Doctrine and Covenants: Elder Gerald N. Lund's *Hearing the Voice of the Lord*, and Mary Margaret Muller's *The Holy Ghost: The Third Member of the Godhead*. Both thoroughly and authoritatively explain the workings of the Spirit and how to cultivate this spiritual gift and guide.

Recommendations from the President of the Sunday School

In the October 2006 General Conference Elder Roger A. Merrill, then Sunday School General President and former Franklin-Covey executive, talked about receiving knowledge by the Spirit. The following are three recommendations that he made in this regard.

> In our Church meetings, in our personal and family scripture study, and even this day as we listen to the Lord's prophets and apostles, some of us will receive more than others. Why? I am learning that those who truly receive do at least three things that others may not do.
>
> First, they *seek*. . . . When we focus . . . on seeking and receiving the Spirit, we become less concerned about a teacher or speaker holding our attention and more concerned about giving our attention to the Spirit. Remember, *receive* is a verb. It is a principle of action. It is a fundamental expression of faith."[4]

He shares this in the context of attending a Sunday School class. But the principle can also easily be applied to when we are reading the scriptures, as he notes:

> Second, those who receive, *feel.* While revelation comes to the mind and heart, it is most often felt. Until we learn to pay attention to these spiritual feelings, we usually do not even recognize the Spirit.
>
> In a recent conversation I had with one of our daughters-in-law, she suggested that we can help even young children become aware of these feelings of the Spirit. We can ask them questions such as, "How do you feel as we read this scripture together? What do you feel the Spirit is prompting you to do?" These are good questions for us all. They demonstrate the desire to receive.
>
> Third, those who receive by the Spirit *intend to act.* As the prophet Moroni instructed, to receive a witness of the Book of Mormon, we must ask "with real intent" (Moroni 10:4). The Spirit teaches when we honestly intend to do something about what we learn."[5]

I thought those plain words were powerful counsel. Perhaps I paid better attention to this address because I knew and greatly admired Elder Merrill's father. He was once my stake president and later my home teaching companion. No doubt the Spirit has guided this family in their scripture study and life's decisions, as it can guide us if we will follow this counsel.

Forgetting Is also a Gift

In addition to the admonitions to remember, in the Doctrine and Covenants there are two notes about the value of forgetting. In section 9 the Lord suggests there are some choices or sins that are just best to forget, and that the Spirit can aid us in forgetting, giving us a "stupor of thought"—so that we cannot remember that which is wrong (v. 9). What a blessing it would be if we could forget everything that was wrong—misunderstandings, misinterpretations, false ideas about the world or ourselves, things we have done wrong, or times when others have wronged us.

Many of us experience this stupor of thought from time to time, but we seldom think of it as a spiritual gift. Those with Alzheimer's disease are a typical example. But even in this case, forgetting some things can be a blessing. Often caregivers (usually spouses and other family members) are bothered more by what the person with dementia can remember than by what they forget. It can be frustrating when loved ones can't remember your name or the names of family members, when they last took their medicine, or when they can't remember the doctor informing them it is no longer safe to drive. But it can be even worse when they remember some traumatic event from the past, and they think they or other family members are in danger now. Or they may remember their children are in school and feel they need to go pick them up. In such cases, some additional forgetting can be a blessing. And by redirecting them to other memories, the caregiver relies on the impaired person's ability to forget to help them through the day.

Forgive and Forget

For those of us without memory impairment, some forgetting, as well as some forgiving, may be a blessing. The Lord notes His ability and willingness to forget. One of the most comforting verses in all scripture is in D&C 58:42, where the Lord says, "Behold, he who has repented of his sins, the same is forgiven, and I, the Lord, *remember them no more*" (emphasis added). Here the Lord equates forgiving with forgetting. And ample evidence suggests this is truly the case.

I am a member of the Salt Lake chapter of the International Association for Near-Death Studies (IANDS). Each month we invite individuals who have had near-death experiences to come and share with us what they have learned. Recently, LDS author Ranelle Wallace shared with us her out-of-body experience after being burned in a plane crash. As is often the case, during her experience she was shown what is called a "life review." As she notes in her book, The Burning Within,

Ranelle was pleased, though not surprised, as she reviewed the various events of her life. Those distressing events she was not proud of, but had repented of, were not included in her life review.

What a comforting thought that is—the Lord will truly no longer remember the things we have repented of. And if the Lord is willing to forgive and forget, shouldn't we? Certainly that has been His counsel.6

As we prepare to study and remember the teachings of the Doctrine and Covenants, are there things that would be best for us to forget? What might they be?

- Past offenses of others
- Past failings or shortcomings, both of ourselves and others
- Erroneous ideas we may have picked up growing up
- Game times of Sunday afternoon football

History is replete with the fact that, like ancient Israel in the Old Testament, the Pharisees in the New Testament, and Laman and Lemuel in the Book of Mormon, we tend to forget the things that are right and remember too well the things that are wrong. The Doctrine and Covenants suggests that the Spirit can help us reverse those tendencies.

In addition to inviting the Spirit to help us remember, it would be appropriate to ask for His help to forget those things that are wrong or do not edify us.

A Revelation with a Promise

My friend Dr. Robert Morrow, a former orthopedic surgeon, notes that the Doctrine and Covenants suggests another interesting way to tap into the influence and insights of the Holy Spirit and improve our memory. That is to live in full obedience to the Word of Wisdom (see chapter 6 for details). Many people think they are in compliance with the Word of Wisdom when they are not. For example, how many of us eat meat (the flesh of fowl or beasts) "only in times of winter, or of cold, or famine" (D&C 89:12)?

The Word of Wisdom talks about healthy bones. Dr. Morrow notes, "Those who abide by this counsel have significantly stronger bones, and lower levels of cancer, than those who do not." However, on a more spiritual plane he drew attention to the final promise of the Word of Wisdom, which states, "And all saints who remember to keep and do these sayings, walking in obedience to the commandments, shall receive [not only] health in their navel and marrow to their bones; [But also they] shall find wisdom and great treasures of knowledge, even hidden treasures" (D&C 89:18–19).

Dr. Morrow uses the prophet Daniel as an example. Daniel restricted his diet to pulse (plants bearing seeds, nuts, and grains) and water, with no meat or wine. As a result Daniel and his brethren were declared to be ten times brighter than all the other wise men in the kingdom. Plus he was able to receive revelations from the Lord to interpret the king's dreams and make wise recommendations for the king's realm. Dr. Morrow believes, "Our spirituality may be adversely affected by the amount of meat we consume."

In other words, as Parley P. Pratt noted in *A Voice of Warning and Instruction to All People*, following the Word of Wisdom may enable us to be more open to receiving the gifts of the Spirit. This includes inspiration and revelation from God to guide us and our families, not only in our study of the scriptures, but also in the affairs of our lives.

NOTES

1. D&C 52:14; see also 50:1.

2. Elden J. Watson, *The Manuscript History of Brigham Young 1846–1847,* 529 (23 Feb. 1847 entry). Quoted in Robert L. Millet, *Alive in Christ: The Miracle of Spiritual Rebirth,* 200–201.

3. *Teachings of the Presidents of the Church: Wilford Woodruff,* 46.

4. Merrill, A. Roger, "Receiving by the Spirit," *Ensign*, Nov. 2006, 92–94.

5. Ibid.

6. See D&C 64:7, 9–10, 13; D&C 98: 39–45

3

PRACTICAL ADVICE FROM THE DOCTRINE AND COVENANTS FOR IMPROVING MEMORY

"That your bodies and your minds may be invigorated."
—D&C 88:124

Most books that talk about improving memory either talk about methods and techniques for getting the most from our memory (regardless of its health or condition), or about food, nutrients, or drugs for improving organic memory (the gray matter) including the cells, neurons, membranes, and synapses of the brain. I try to make my readers aware of things in both aspects they can take and do to improve memory. Not only does that make sense, it's essential if we want to enjoy optimal mental ability and the fruits of a lifetime of learning and remembering.

In the following chapters you will explore various methods and strategies for learning and making the most of your memory, so you can better remember the Doctrine and Covenants and Church history. First though, there are two relatively new and important insights for maintaining and enhancing organic memory.

New Hope for the Brain

There is a new term called "neuroplasticity." It emphasizes the interdependency between the organic structures of the brain and efforts to acquire and retain new information. Neuroplasticity refers to the brain's ability to rebuild and reshape itself. Scientists who study the brain once believed there were limits to the number of neurons or brain cells that a person could develop. The belief was that this was determined at birth or shortly thereafter, but certainly by the time we reached age thirty. Along with this, they have long known that as we age, especially over age fifty, the brain tends to slow down and shrink.

Brain researchers, therefore, were quite surprised to find in recent years that the brain is constantly rebuilding itself, and that individuals, even in their seventies and eighties, can still grow new neurons and extensions, called dendrites. Even in some cases when there has been brain damage, investigators have found that the brain has the ability to essentially rewire itself and reconnect around the damage. This is neuroplasticity in action.

Neuroplasticity can give new hope to those experiencing an increasing number of "senior moments." But it also provides motivation to master the concepts in this book and improve our understanding of and memory for the events in Church history and the teachings of the Doctrine and Covenants.

Some of the best evidence for neuroplasticity was found in the Nun Study.[1] This study began in the early nineties when a group of 678 nuns agreed to join a study on aging and Alzheimer's disease, conducted by Dr. David Snowdon from the University of Kentucky. One of Snowdon's most fascinating finds was that some nuns died with Alzheimer's, as evidenced by autopsies, but did not show the typical signs of memory loss. Why?

These nuns had stayed the most mentally active, learning and sharing new things even as they grew older. Most of them had been teachers. Not only had they continued teaching, even into their seventies, but more important, they continued learning and using their brains.

This process of acquiring and communicating knowledge appears to both promote new brain cell growth and provide potent protection against memory deterioration in later years. A recent major European study found "the most effective neuroprotective therapy . . . may well not be a pill, but education and intellectual activity."[2]

Another important, relevant finding from the Nun Study and other studies of brain health is that those whose language tends to be imprecise or nonspecific seem more vulnerable to later cognitive decline. New research suggests that by being more precise in the words we use to describe things and events, we might be able to better protect our brain and memories from fading—not to mention the value of this for improving interaction and the quality of life.[3]

In light of this, when you think of the teachings in the Doctrine and Covenants and Church history, are your memories precise or are they fuzzy? Do you know the sequence of events in Church history, such as what was revealed when and why? Do you know the dates of important events? Can you identify what doctrines are in which sections? Can you recall or quote your favorite teachings and verses verbatim, or are your descriptions of doctrines and ideas quite vague?

If we were more precise in our gospel knowledge, wouldn't it help to be less vulnerable to spiritual decline as well?

Science Supports Modern Revelation

What scientists are learning about the brain's need to be involved in lifelong learning supports doctrines revealed during the Restoration. A common question in the world is, "What is the purpose of our existence in mortality?" Sadly for some, without the concept of divine design, they may not see a purpose to their existence. Some, such as theists, tend to see humans as Tinkertoys of God, designed for His good pleasure. The restored gospel, however, provides the added insight that life is about learning and growing—eternal progression. From these revelations we learn that we were involved in this pursuit of knowledge even before we came to earth, and we will continue in the hereafter.

Joseph Smith noted, "Knowledge saves a man; and in the world of spirits no man can be exalted but by knowledge."[4] Later he was instructed, "Whatever principle of intelligence we attain unto in this life, it will rise with us in the resurrection. And if a person gains more knowledge and intelligence in this life through his diligence and obedience than another, he will have so much the advantage in the world to come" (D&C 130:18–19). Moreover, the Lord revealed, "The glory of God is intelligence, or, in other words, light and truth" (D&C 93:36). Optimally in mortality we learn and grow in light and truth to become more like our Father in Heaven (see 2 Peter 1:3–5; Matthew 5:48).

Is it any wonder then that the Lord designed our brains for lifelong learning? Not only is learning essential for eternal progression, but from a scientific perspective it is a neurological imperative for the health and well-being of our brain. If we are not involved in fulfilling this purpose of lifelong learning and growing, our brain will atrophy. It's as if God said, "I have given you a brain designed to enable you to fulfill your purposes in mortality—to learn, grow, and gain experience. Use it or lose it!"

Sleep on It

Our brain has the basic need for sleep. According to Cornell University psychology professor James B. Maas, sleeping less than a normal night's sleep (seven to nine hours) negatively impacts memory, learning, thinking, alertness, creativity, health, longevity, and quality of life.[5]

In 2001 the National Institute of Health initiated a campaign to encourage children to get more sleep: "There is a growing body of scientific evidence showing that inadequate sleep results in tiredness, difficulties with focused attention, irritability, easy frustration, and difficulty modulating impulses and emotions. This is as true for children as it is for adults."[6]

Dr. Layne Hermansen, a general practioner in Draper, Utah, notes that "a college-aged adult needs at least 7½ to 8½ hours of sleep per night in order to maintain proper cognition. . . . And to maintain good grades."[7] Regarding physical health, he states "Sleep deprivation . . . provokes the body to become less sensitive to insulin. This in turn can cause weight gain, high blood pressure and diabetes. A lack of sleep also stresses the body, which can result in heart attacks and strokes later in life. There are also higher levels of anxiety and depression among the sleep deprived."[8] Moreover, he added, "The brain's frontal cortex relies on sleep to function effectively. Insufficient rest adversely affects the frontal cortex's ability to control speech, access memory, and solve problems."[9]

We now know chronic sleep deprivation can also increase the risk for dementia as we grow older.

The notion that sleep is important for learning has been debated by scientists for years. Recently, however, advances in neuroscience led researchers to study both humans and animals and sleep, which provide clear evidence that sleep is indeed important for memory and learning.

"In one recent example, participants had to repeatedly type a sequence on a keyboard. A group trained in the morning and then tested 12 hours later showed no significant improvement. But a full night's sleep improved their performance by almost 20 percent."[10]

Sleep not only prevents interference from other material, but may also allow the brain to reprocess newly learned information so that memories stick better. This is particularly the case with deeper REM (Rapid Eye Movement) sleep.[11]

You may have heard that it is a good idea to get a good night's sleep before a big test. However, new research suggests that it may also be important to get a good night's sleep *after* you study or after you practice a skill such as playing a musical instrument.

One fascinating study of brain cell activity in zebra finches revealed that during sleep these birds replay songs in their heads, possibly to help secure the memory of them.[12] Humans may do something similar.

This reminds me of a conversation I had with Elder Vaughan J. Featherstone a few years ago. Elder Featherstone (now an emeritus General Authority) was well-known for his outstanding memory and ability to recite poetry. I asked him how he was able to do that so well. "Practice," he said. He noted it wasn't easy for him either, but one thing that seemed to help was rehearsing at bedtime. Sometimes even after he went to bed he would go over verses in his head. Now science suggests there is good reason for his doing so.

To summarize the research we now know:

- The brain can continue learning and growing at any age.
- The brain needs mental stimulation to stay healthy.
- The brain consolidates and practices what we learned during the day after we go to sleep.
- Learning continues to take place while we are asleep.
- Sleep after a lesson is learned may help the brain consolidate and better retain that new knowledge.

How to Get a Good Night's Sleep

Stating the importance of sleep can be easier than securing it, especially as we grow older. Here are ten suggestions from the experts in the field.

1. Exercise twenty to thirty minutes a day, but avoid exercising three to five hours prior to bedtime. Experiments show the more physical exercise an animal does, the more REM sleep an animal will have. Exercising three to five hours prior to bedtime can increase metabolism and inhibit sleep.

2. Don't eat a heavy meal before going to bed. Avoid meat for supper. A meal of pasta or other carbohydrates may help.

3. Eat foods high in tryptophan earlier in the day like tofu, flax or pumpkin seeds, gluten flour, almonds, walnuts, soybeans, black-eyed peas, brown rice, halibut, mackerel, or turkey.

4. Relax before going to bed—take a warm bath or shower or read to ease into a sleep routine.

5. See bright light first thing in the morning; it helps rebalance circadian rhythms to overcome insomnia.

6. Eat and go to bed at the same time each night.

7. Control your room temperature.

8. Make sure your room is dark at night. Turn off any radio or other night lights (light disrupts melatonin production.)

9. Increase calcium, magnesium, and B-vitamin intake.

10. For those over age fifty-five, a melatonin supplement may help. (This is a powerful sleep-inducing hormone and should not be given to children or younger adults.)

Finally, the Lord has told us, "Retire to thy bed early, that ye may not be weary; arise early, that your bodies and your minds may be invigorated" (D&C 88:124).

University studies have shown that students who get more sleep before midnight tend to get better grades. Two hours of sleep before midnight may be better than four extra hours in the morning.[13] Try it and see if it doesn't improve your memory.

NOTES

1. University of Kentucky Chandler Medical Center, "Scientific." http://www.mc.uky.edu/nunnet/scientific.htm. This website lists many studies and findings resulting from the Nun Study, such as,

   Snowdon DA. "Aging and Alzheimer's disease: Lessons from the Nun Study." *The Gerontologist* 37(2):150–156, 1997.

   Snowdon DA. and Riley KP: "Professor Snowdon replies." *The Gerontologist* 38:5–6, 1998.

2. R. de la Fuente-Fernandez. "Impact of Neuroprotection on Incidence of Alzheimer's Disease." Quoted from Medical

News Today. "Education—The Best Pill of All For Preventing Alzheimer's." www.medicalnewstoday.com/medicalnews.php?newsid=59612.

3. JA Mortimer et al. "Very early detection of Alzheimer neuropathology and the role of brain reserve in modifying its clinical expression." *Journal of Geriatric Psychiatry and Neurology* 18(4):218-223, 2005.

4. Joseph Smith, *History of The Church of Jesus Christ of Latter-day Saints*, 6:314.

5. J. B. Maas, *Power Sleep* (New York: Villard Books, 1998).

6. Press release July 16, 2001. Star Sleeper, "NHLBI'S Children and Sleep Campaign Promotes Adequate Sleep for the New School Year." www.nhlbi.nih.gov/new/press/01-02-07.htm.

7. BYU Newsnet: News from the Y. "Sleep Crucial to Grades," Kristen Radford. 13 Mar 2007. http://newsnet.byu.edu/story.cfm/63515.

8. Ibid.

9. Ibid.

10. Society for Neuroscience, Brain Briefings. SfN, "Sleeping and Learning," April 2003. http://www.sfn.org/index.cfm?pagename=brainBriefings_sleepAndLearning.

11. P. Maquet et al. "Experience-dependent changes in cerebral activation during human REM sleep," Nature Neuroscience, 3:831–836, 2000. Online: www.nature.com/neuro/journal/v3/n8/abs/nn0800_831.html

12. University Of Chicago Medical Center. "Singing Silently During Sleep Helps Birds Learn Songs," *ScienceDaily*. 31 October, 2000. Available at www.sciencedaily.com/releases/2000/10/001031065529.htm.

13. Reported by Neil Nedley, *Depression Recovery Program* (Ardmore, OK: Nedley Publishing, 2006).

4

THE LAWS AND PRINCIPLES OF MEMORY

When asked how he governed his people, Joseph Smith said, "I teach them correct principles and they govern themselves."[1] Similarly, in order to effectively govern our mind and our memories, it is helpful if we understand the principles and processes related to how the mind and memory work. People who have outstanding recall abilities either consciously or unconsciously apply these principles and what I call "the seven habits of highly effective learners." These habits are built upon the foundation principles of effective memory—the principles that govern the storage and retrieval of information in the brain.

Most people understand what a habit is, but fewer understand the nature and value of principles. So let's review a few definitions. A "principle" is defined in the American edition of the Oxford desk dictionary as:

1. A fundamental truth or law as the basis of reasoning and action.
2. A law of nature or science.

This may remind you of D&C 130:21: "And when we obtain any blessing from God, it is by obedience to that law upon which it is predicated."

Therefore, if you want to "obtain" or develop a good memory and effectively recall insights and lessons from the Doctrine and Covenants and Church history, first gain a clear understanding of the laws or principles upon which a good memory and effective recall are based. Then develop habits which are aligned with those principles.

A principle is defined in behavioral science as "a statement about the relationship between two variables." A variable is something that changes—increases or decreases, gets stronger or weaker—such as our ability to recall what we have read. Typically this describes how a change in one variable (some action or behavior) affects another variable (the result). In other words, a principle is how a change in A affects B. For example, one of the most basic principles of memory relates the frequency of rehearsal ability to recall, and can be stated as follows: The more frequently and actively a person rehearses information, the greater his or her ability to remember that information when needed.

Principles, like the definitions suggest, reflect underlying laws of nature. In this case they reflect human nature, and more specifically the nature of how memory works or how it is governed.

Once you understand the principles that govern behaviors or interactions in a given field, it's easier to determine appropriate behaviors in that area—in this case appropriate habits to form for better memory. Moreover, underlying principles can be applied in many different settings and used to develop various methods and techniques that would be effective in new situations. This "rehearsal principle" can be applied to strengthening our ability to recall information from almost any source (reading or lectures, for example) in almost any area of study (such as science, religion, or human relations).

This discussion might seem a bit esoteric for our purposes. After all, this is not a college course, nor is this meant to be a science project. Instead I want to provide a practical guide for you. I hope you will soon see how this all relates and how the following concepts, principles, habits, and methods can be helpful in improving your ability to remember.

First we will review seven principles and habits that seem most relevant for improving memory. Then we will explore how these might apply more specifically to remembering the contents and chronology of the Doctrine and Covenants and Church history. If you learn and apply these, you will be amazed at how much more effective you will be in governing your memory.

The A RECORD Formula

Most of the basic principles for improving memory processes can be summed up with the acronym A RECORD. If you want to remember something you just have to make A RECORD. Using the first letter of the words you want to remember to form another word (an acronym) to help remind you of each of these words is one of many methods we will review to help facilitate recall.

What I did not know when I developed that acronym and wrote *How to Remember Everything in the Old Testament* was that *record* has an older, deeper association with remembering. We tend to think of a record as a written record, but in the beginning it was not so. In an article titled "What's in a Word? Etymology!" Cynthia L. Hallen notes, "to 're-cord' is to *learn things by heart so that we can ponder them again and again*. Records of personal and family history enable our children to 're-member' and 're-turn' to us. Scriptural records . . . enable righteous forebears to speak directly to the hearts of their descendants."[2]

The following are seven principles and habits contained in the A RECORD formula. Then we will review a few techniques for applying and optimizing these principles.

The first A in this formula stands for *attention.* If you want to remember something, it's going to cost you. You will have to "pay" attention. In order to remember wisdom from the Doctrine and Covenants or inspiring stories from Church history, you must first focus on and attend to what is being said. Most of the time when we forget a verse of scripture or other bits of information, it is not a problem with our memory or retrieval system. We just didn't pay close enough attention when the information was presented.

Despite what you may have heard about subliminal learning, the brain and working memory do not effectively store everything that goes on around us or passes through our field of vision (though our mind and spirit may). In order to remember something specific, we must first focus our attention and then get involved with that information. Generally we can only store those things that we pay close attention to for long-term retrieval. Highlighting or circling key words is one way to sharpen our attention. This principle and its associated habit are stated as follows:

The Attention Principle: The more attention you pay to what you read or hear, the easier it will be to remember.

The Attention Habit: Pay close attention to, and get involved with, the material you wish to remember.

The other six principles, you will see, all reinforce attention and involvement.

The first R in RECORD stands for *relate.* Some experts feel this is the real key to effective storage and retrieval. As you read or hear new information, you will find that it generally sticks best when you can relate or associate this in some memorable way with something else that you already know or have stored.

Perhaps this is why the Lord encouraged the Saints in section 109 to "seek ye out of the best books words of wisdom" (v. 7). The more we know, the more we can relate and connect new information.

This is one reason why those who are older sometimes retain new information better than those who are younger. They can relate to it better. They have more information and experiences to which they can tie or associate new information. This causes the new information to be more meaningful to them, which in turn helps them pay better attention. It leads them to becoming more involved in developing an image or related association that will clearly stick in long-term memory.

Most memory training methods, strategies, or techniques are ways people have developed to help them relate or associate new information to more familiar knowledge. This is usually done with vivid memorable picture associations, relating the new information with things they already know well. This enables them to better recall the new information.

The Relate Principle: The more we can relate new information to past easily recalled information, the easier it will be to remember the new information.

The Relate Habit: Relate new information in memorable ways (concrete, easily envisioned) with past familiar and easily recalled information.

In chapter 5 we will review methods for relating the sections and teachings of the Doctrine and Covenants with other things you are familiar with, and to recall the location of important teachings in the Doctrine and Covenants and the dates of important events in Church history.

The E in this formula stands for *envision*. Most people have better visual memories than auditory memories. For most of us, we remember events, concepts, and ideas better if we can picture, visualize, or recreate them in our minds. Most of us remember pictures of a scene better than verbal descriptions of it. We also tend to remember things we read better than things we hear, especially if a picture, diagram, chart, or other graphic visual aid is included. I find it is easier to remember the events of Church history if I can vividly picture them. Even teachings from the Doctrine and Covenants are easier to recall if I can see the larger picture or setting in which they were given.

The envision principle and the associated habit to be formed can be stated as follows:

The Envision Principle: The more vividly you can envision or picture what you read or hear, the easier it will be to remember when you need it.

The Envision Habit: Envision or picture what you wish to remember, with as much sensory-rich detail and as vividly as you can.

The C stands for *concrete*. Concrete objects are much easier to visualize and thus remember than are abstract concepts or ideas. Perhaps that is one reason, if not the primary reason, why the Lord instituted the emblems of the sacrament. These are concrete, tangible reminders of Him and His sacrifice for us. And so we take, eat, and drink these emblems in remembrance of Him.

Because concrete symbols are easier to envision and remember than concepts, society uses graphic letters and words to represent ideas, just as computer systems use icons or pictures to represent programs. Icons make it easier to identify the program and recall the needed information.

For most of us, our natural memories are pretty good. Like computers, we just need a concrete clue, hint, or symbol to remind us and enable us to access and pull up a more complete memory. So you may want to develop symbols of concrete objects to represent concepts you are trying to remember in the Doctrine and Covenants.

Missionaries are often encouraged to memorize section 4, which lists a variety of qualities that are important for success in the work of the Lord. Some of these qualities, like faith, virtue, knowledge, temperance, and patience, are abstract concepts that may be hard to envision, and thus difficult to remember. However, if you can create a concrete symbol for each quality, you will find them easier to picture, link, and recall at will. For example, you might envision seeds to represent faith, a rose to represent virtue, a book for knowledge, duct tape for temperance, and a nurse for patience, or something else that reminds you of these qualities.

The associated principle and habit here can be stated as follows:

The Concrete Principle: The more you picture concrete visible symbols (rather than less tangible concepts or ideas), the easier it will be to remember.

The Concrete Habit: Picture more concrete objects as symbols to represent less tangible concepts or ideas.

The O stands for *organize,* or put in *order*. In the Doctrine and Covenants we are told to "organize yourselves" (D&C 109:8). If you want a good memory you need to follow that counsel. Good memories are organized memories. Paul said that "God is not the author of confusion" (1 Corinthians 14:33). Nor should you be about the things you want to commit to memory.

Like any file or retrieval system, if you want to find what you want when you want it from your memory bank, you will need to enter it in an organized manner first. Order makes access and retrieval much easier. As an example, the Doctrine and Covenants is organized in sections by numbers. Generally, these sections are chronological in accordance with the events of the Church. This ordering and numbering system makes it easier to organize and remember this information.

This principle can be stated as follows:

The Organize Principle: The more you organize information in ways that are meaningful to you, the easier it will be for you to remember.

The Organizing Habit: Organize what you wish to remember in ways that are meaningful to and memorable for you.

The second R stands for *repeat, rehearse,* or *reiterate*. Repetition is considered to be the mother of memory. I prefer to use the verb *rehearse* in this formula because it suggests a more involved and dynamic process. Rehearsal sessions ideally should be set up within a few minutes after learning new information, then again within the hour, after a few hours, that evening, the next day, a few days later, a week later, and as needed thereafter. This spaced rehearsal is the key to long-term storage and recall. The Lord uses this principle in His Church. We are to attend meetings regularly, partake of the sacrament often, and study the scriptures daily. Perhaps this is why we have the four standard works that teach the same principles over and over. The more often we hear, see, and recall them to mind, the more deeply ingrained in our brain and behavior they become, so that we remember to apply these in our daily lives when needed.

There is a principle in educational and behavioral psychology called "over learning." Studies related to this suggest that the more we "over learn" a process or information, the easier it will be to access and apply. Perhaps that is what the Lord is trying to do with us through the various Church programs. He wants us to learn the gospel so well that application becomes automatic.

The Rehearsal Principle: The more frequently and actively you rehearse information, the greater your ability to remember that information when you need it.

The Rehearsal Habit: Actively rehearse what you have learned at regular intervals.

Here is one way to rehearse any new information. Fold a regular piece of notebook paper down the middle. On the outside fold, write questions on the material you want to recall. On the inside of the fold, write the answers. During rehearsal sessions, look at the questions and see if you can recall the answers. If you have difficulty in recalling any of the answers, you may want to review the above-noted principles for insights on what you could do differently. Then, using A RECORD as a guide, plus the following ideas and those in chapter 5, develop a strategy and cues to plant that information more vividly into your memory. It's also helpful to make a note of your memory cues or clues on the opposite side of the inner fold.

The D is for *deliver*. We could call this the "deliver paradox." After you receive and record new information, if you really want to retain it you've got to give it away. Deliver a lesson or lecture on it; or in other words, share this information with others. And when there is nobody around to share it with, you can deliver it out loud to yourself, as if you were delivering it to others. When people deliver to others what they have learned it deepens that knowledge in themselves. It's like a testimony—the more you share it, the stronger and more firmly implanted it becomes.

The teachings of the Book of Mormon and the new revelations given to the Church were reinforced in the minds of the early missionaries as they shared the gospel. The same is true today. Accordingly, the more you deliver or share with others what you learn from the Doctrine and Covenants and Church history, the more deeply these will become imbedded in your own memories.

The Lord gives an interesting promise in D&C 88:78: "Teach ye diligently and my grace shall attend you, that you may be instructed more perfectly in theory, in principle, in doctrine, in the law of the gospel, in all things that pertain unto the kingdom of God, that are expedient for you to understand."

The Lord says that when we teach diligently, by the grace of God, we are "instructed more perfectly." Teaching facilitates the teacher's learning.

Most teachers will tell you that they learn much more in preparing and delivering their lessons than their students do. First, they have to pay closer attention, get more involved, relate it to other information, and make it clearer. Second, through rehearsal and delivery the information is burned more deeply into their memory. I remember learning this principle once in Primary when I had to give a two-and-a-half minute talk on one of my pioneer ancestors. I found I learned a lot more from that experience than when I just sat and heard other kids give their talks. It's a true principle and can be stated as follows.

The Deliver Principle: The more you deliver or share what you have learned, the greater will be your ability to remember that information when needed.

The Deliver Habit: Deliver or share new information that you have learned with others, or at least deliver it to yourself, in a dramatic or memorable way.

The Seven Principles for Making a Memorable RECORD

In review, the A RECORD formula and principles are as follows.

A is for *attention*

The more attention you pay to what you see or hear, the easier it will be to remember.

R is for *Relate*

The more you relate new information to past, easily recalled information, the easier it will be to remember.

E is for *Envision*

The more vividly you can envision or picture what you read or hear, the easier it will be to remember.

C is for *Concrete*

The more you picture concrete visible objects (rather than less tangible concepts or ideas), the easier it will be to remember.

O is for *Organize*

The more you organize information in ways that are meaningful to you, the easier it will be for you to remember.

R is for *Rehearse*

The more frequently and actively you rehearse information, the greater your ability to remember that information.

D is for *Deliver*

The more you deliver or share what you have learned, the greater your ability to remember that information.

How to Remember the "A RECORD" Formula

It is important to cement this formula into your brain, because these seven principles provide the foundation you will need for the procedures and techniques that follow. Moreover, if you experience some difficulty in recalling information from your studies, these can provide a good checklist for troubleshooting. With an awareness of these principles you can add your own memory techniques as needed.

Since an awareness of each principle is essential to understanding what follows, take a few minutes right now to commit them to memory. Make sure this acronym and its related principles are firmly fixed in your long-term memory before you go on. To do this, apply the principles and methods we have just learned.

If you've read to this point, at least you've been giving this formula a significant amount of **attention**. Plus you have **related** or tied the acronym A RECORD to its associated principles. If you have also **envisioned** or pictured yourself doing these things as we went along, that should have helped to etch them into your brain, especially if your images were **concrete** enough. You see that by relating these principles to the acronym, you have an **organized** way to remember them. Plus you will note that they are organized sequentially; whenever you remember something you will typically go through this process in this order. In fact, that is the major habit for learning that you need to rehearse over and again. Then **deliver it** to or share it with someone else.

By now you should have it stored fairly well. But just to make sure, here is an exercise to try. Once you've read these instructions, put down this book, and on the left-hand side of a blank sheet of paper, write this acronym vertically as follows:

A
R
E
C
O
R
D

If you can't remember all seven letters think of this clue phrase: "In order for me to remember what I read in the Doctrine and Covenants or Church history, I must be like Joseph's scribe and make A RECORD of those things that I wish to remember."

From memory, write what each letter stands for. If you miss a principle, look it up, but then put the book down and write it from memory.

Now, turn the paper over and think of the acronym clue phrase again. Then write down the letters vertically, as noted above. Next, note to the right what each stands for and as much of its associated principle as you can recall. As you do this, envision yourself doing each step with some information you are learning or would like to remember from the Doctrine and Covenants. When you are done you should have this acronym and these seven principles of memory chiseled into your brain. To make sure the image doesn't fade, do this little exercise once more after you are done with this chapter, and then again before bed, tomorrow, the next day, and at least once next week and each week thereafter for the next month. By then it will be well in mind and ready to apply any time, any place, and anywhere.

The Seven Habits of Effective Learners in Review

1. The Attention Habit: Pay close attention to, and get involved with, those things that you wish to remember.

2. The Relate Habit: Relate new information in memorable ways (concrete, easily envisioned) with past familiar and easily recalled information.

3. The Envision Habit: Envision or picture what you wish to remember with as much sensory rich detail and as vividly as you can.

4. The Concrete Habit: Picture more concrete objects or symbols to represent less tangible concepts or ideas.

5. The Organizing Habit: Organize what you wish to remember in ways that are meaningful to and memorable for you.

6. The Rehearsal Habit: Actively rehearse what you have learned at regular intervals as needed.

7. The Deliver Habit: Deliver or share new information that you have learned with others, or at least deliver it to yourself, in a dramatic or memorable way.

Optimizing Memories

If you have ever seen someone perform an amazing memory feat, you've seen the power of these principles in action and the potential of a trained memory. Some typical examples might be remembering everyone's name and birth date in a large audience, remembering a twenty-plus digit number in perfect order, or describing the contents of every page in a magazine. How do they accomplish these seemingly miraculous feats? Such individuals are likely either savants, or they are ordinary people like you and me who know the following methods for optimizing memories.

These memory masters, or mnemonists as they are sometimes called, accomplish their feats by employing the A RECORD principles and utilizing the following strategies in applying those principles.[3] Most of these strategies are based upon one or more of the principles, particularly the envision and relate principles, and are simple ways to make these processes more powerful.

Extraordinary but Not Profane

Joseph Smith was able to accurately recount what the angel Moroni taught him in his room, as recorded in the Pearl of Great Price, because this visitation was so extraordinary. It was also rehearsed three times—the second R principle. Most books on memory suggest that for an association to be vivid or most memorable it needs to be bizarre, farcical, zany, exaggerated, or distorted— anything but ordinary.

However, when trying to remember concepts or teachings of salvation from scripture, these image qualities just don't seem appropriate. They might even be considered profane or sacrilegious. On the other hand, the idea that unusual or extraordinary things are more easily remembered is undeniable.

As noted in the envision principle, we remember stories and ideas much better if we can envision them in our minds. Here are ten less bizarre, but no less effective, ways to make these mental pictures and associations more memorable.

1. **Anchor** your images to a specific location. If you can envision the location of different events in Church history, and see those each time in those same settings, they will be easier to find in your mind and to recall. Additionally, you can envision doctrines from the Doctrine and Covenants being presented or acted out in specific settings in New York, Ohio, or Missouri. Or you can imagine them being acted out in your neighborhood or community. Tying memories to specific locations can greatly facilitate ease of recall.

2. **Amplify** aspects of what you want to remember by making them larger, longer, taller, wider, or in some other way more exaggerated than normal. In D&C 1:13 it states that the sword of the Lord "shall fall upon the inhabitants of the earth." An image of a four-hundred-foot sword falling horizontally on an unrighteous mob (like Dorothy's house in *The Wizard of Oz*), would likely be more memorable than an image of a three-foot-sword falling to the ground.

3. **Create action and interaction** in your images of the text. See things rising, falling, twisting, jerking, expanding, shrinking, and so forth. Most people remember when Joseph was tarred and feathered and had his tooth chipped as the mob tried to poison him. This is most memorable because of the action in the images involved. Likewise the fighting at Haun's Mill suggests images that are not easily forgotten because of the action and interactions involved.

But you can also use this to bring more abstract lessons to life. Section 121 talks about covering sins; gratifying pride; and exercising control, dominion, or compulsion upon the souls of the children of men. Imagine how that interaction might look—literally covering up sins with dirt or a blanket, spending large amount of money for bigger and better things, physically controlling others with leashes. If when you read you can envision the various actions involved, they will be more memorable. What does it mean to gratify pride? It may take some thought and creativity, even study. But it can be fun to create associated images, and you will not soon forget such pictures nor the concepts they represent.

4. **Add color** to your images. The brain likes color. Adding color to your images will help stimulate the neurons of memory and make for a more memorable picture and easier recall.

5. **Create unusual, extraordinary, or unconventional** images or associations. Some of these are built in to Church history already. Golden plates are unusual, as are the Urim and Thummim and reading through a hat. Newel Knight's demon possession with his "limbs distorted and twisted in every shape and appearance,"[4] was extraordinary. Many Church doctrines, like the appearing of angels, ordinances for the dead, and the deification of man may seem unconventional. See the number pegs system in chapter 5 for additional illustrations of how this technique can be used to remember the location of information and timing of events.

6. **See yourself in the scenes**. Get involved. Imagine that you are there with the Saints as they struggled to build the temple in Kirtland, fled Missouri, drained the swamps in Nauvoo, and crossed the plains. Be there—see and feel the events and interactions as they occur.

7. **Use symbols** or easily visualized objects to represent common concepts. See examples under the concrete principle. Other examples might be picturing a judge's gavel as the symbol for justice, his handshake as symbolic of mercy, a man kneeling with head bowed as a symbol of humility, and a mother's hug or the giving of food as symbolic of charity. For additional symbols, visit a temple and examine its facade.

Develop and use your own creative images and symbols to make effective associations. Mine and those of others may be helpful, but those that you create yourself will likely be most memorable. The more involved you become in developing your own symbols, the more you will remember.

8. **Draw pictures and symbols** to represent the concepts you want to remember the most. You don't have to be an Arnold Friberg. Stick figures work just fine; pen or pencil doodles are great as long as you know what they stand for. These are especially helpful

for visual learners, but also for those who are more right-brained, those with greater tactile sensitivity, and other creative individuals. (See ARECORD4LDS.com for additional applications of this technique.)

9. **Involve other senses** of sound, touch, taste, and even smell in your imagery. By recalling a certain feel, taste, or smell, you can evoke associated memories. Some people naturally experience these senses more than others, but even if you are sensory challenged to some degree, by adding or imagining these other senses in your mental pictures, you can help bring the events of Church history more to life and make your images more memorable. Can you imagine what Liberty Jail must have smelled like? What did the swamps of Nauvoo feel like with all those mosquitoes, or malaria?

You can also amplify the imagery with emotion. If you can deeply empathize with those in Church history and feel related emotions, their experiences will be more memorable for you. Can you imagine how Joseph must have felt when he lost the manuscript of the Book of Mormon, or when he wrote section 121 from Liberty Jail? Can you imagine how the Saints felt as they left their homes and families? If you can imagine and become emotionally involved with the events described, you will not soon forget them.

10. **If you are more auditory** or verbally oriented, you could enhance your images, or at least your recall of the text, by reading it aloud or recording it and then listening to it as you drive to work. Some research suggests your own voice may be more memorable than someone else's. It would also be helpful to discuss what you have learned on a regular basis with a partner. Discussing what you learned and how you will apply the concepts in your life helps solidify them in your mind. That's why we have Sunday school classes, where teachers are counseled to involve class members, "that all may be edified of all" (D&C 88:122).

Linking Life Together

One of the most important methods for remembering, especially for items or events in sequence, is called "linking." This is based on the Relate principle and the fact that we remember new things best if they are related or associated with things we already know. When you learn something new, you link new information to old information. Once you have that connection down, you add the next piece, and so on. This resembles what is already happening in our heads. Whenever we learn new information, it is linked or connected via neurons and dendrites to what we already have stored.

The key to effective linking is creating clear, memorable images of these connections. The various optimizing techniques we just discussed can aid in this process. Creating and visualizing extraordinary interactions among these various concepts or ideas is what facilitates a recall of the connection.

When reading or watching a story unfold, events are naturally linked sequentially to one another. Such is the case with events in Church history. One event leads to another as the story moves along, so there is little need to actively employ this technique for that purpose. It is most helpful when there is not a natural connection, as is often the case in the Doctrine and Covenants, when a revelation goes from one topic to another. In order to remember all of the main points or teachings in a given section, it may be helpful to link them together with this method.

Section 77 is a good section to illustrate the technique of linking. Joseph asks various questions, and the Lord gives him answers. When linking, it is helpful if you can find a unifying theme or thread. In this section there is a connecting thread in that they are all questions prompted by the book of Revelation, but the topics are generally quite dissimilar, and are as follows:

- the sea of glass
- four beasts
- twenty-four elders
- the seven seals

- various angels sent from God
- sealing of the 144,000
- sounding of trumpets
- timing of events
- the little book that was eaten
- two witnesses

So, in order to remember all of these various questions and topics, you would need to create a picture connecting the various elements. There are endless possibilities; here is the one I came up with.

I imagine an ice skating pond where I skated as a boy. This is my anchor location and represents the sea of glass. Slipping and sliding on this are four strange-looking beasts. I see twenty-four missionaries run in from the sidelines and try to climb on to ride the beasts. The elders are followed by seven seals, the kind you would find in a zoo or circus. They are clapping at this hilarious sight when I hear and feel a great wind. Looking up I see four angels swooping in, followed by another coming in from the east. Beneath them in the distance I see a large herd of white and black something coming. I ask the angels what they are; they say these are the 144,000 high priests who have been sealed as prophesied of by John. (As they get closer I can see these are seals wearing white shirts and suspenders.) The angels then sound their long trumpets. Looking up I see something falling from the sky and crash into the ice. It is a large pocket watch about four feet tall. Stuck to the top is a little book, which one of the elders, a friend of mine named John, proceeds to eat. Two other elders step forth and say, "Hey if you need witnesses, we can say we saw it all, and can prophecy of more to come."

You need a bit of imagination to come up with a picture like this to link together the various topics in this section, but you don't need all of the details. The brain only needs a hint to remind it of what you have read. I know for example, from paying attention to the answers given by the Lord in section 77, that the seven seals refers to thousand-year time periods, not mammals in a zoo.

You see all of the elements in my picture are just easily envisioned symbolic aids to help me remember other details. Is it okay to use odd symbols to represent other things in scripture? You must judge for yourself—but isn't that what John did in the book of Revelation? The only problem is John knew what those symbols meant, but Joseph Smith did not—hence Joseph needed section 77. But hopefully your links are clear and memorable enough, and you review the material often enough, that you won't need another revelation to understand them.

Realize that when you employ one or more of these images or memory enhancement techniques, you are paying closer attention, becoming more involved in your interaction with the text and message, envisioning the events, and relating them to concrete things you are more familiar with. As a result, these events and concepts are better organized in your brain, which will enable you to recall and rehearse them more often. If you consistently apply these principles and techniques, the Doctrine and Covenants and Church history can't help but become more memorable for you.

NOTES

1. Joseph Smith, *Millennial Star* 13 (15 November 1851): 339.

2. These are often referred to as "mnemonic" devices. The term *mnemonic* (pronounced "newmonic") is derived from Mnemosyne, the Greek goddess of memory. The early Greeks invented some of these methods.

3. Cynthis L. Hallen, *What's in a Word? Etymology*! Provo, Utah: FARMS, 2003, 105–107. Available at http://farms.byu.edu/display.php?table=jbm&id=306.

4. *Church History in the Fulness of Times* (Salt Lake City, UT: The Church of Jesus Christ of Latter-day Saints, 1993), 69.

5

HOW TO REMEMBER WHO, WHAT, WHEN, AND WHERE

In order to remember the Doctrine and Covenants and Church history effectively, it will be helpful to remember who said and did what, when these events occurred, and where various teachings can be found in the Doctrine and Covenants.

Names and Places

The method for remembering names is quite simple and is again based on the relate principle. It involves four steps.

1. **Make an association.** Find some part of the name that

you can associate with some person, thing, or action that you are already familiar with. You are no doubt familiar with names like Joseph Smith, Oliver Cowdrey, Martin Harris, and Emma Hale. Let's take another name—Joseph Knight. He was of great help to Joseph and Oliver in the early days. When I think of him I imagine him in star-studded, dark blue overalls. The stars on the dark background remind me of "night," the phonetic equivalent of his last name. I imagine when Joseph Smith meets him he notes, "Hey you have the same name as me." Most names in Church history are fairly easy, so let's take one a bit harder: Drusilla Hendricks, was one of the faithful Quincy refugees who was miraculously saved from starvation. To remember her name you might imagine her drawing a silly picture of a hen doing tricks.

2. **Tie to text.** Tie the words or phrase used to remember the name to some key phrase or idea you want to remember from the text. So you could say, "As she waited to die with only a spoonful of sugar and a saucer of cornmeal, Drusilla Hendricks drew silly pics of a hen doing tricks." Keep in mind you don't need a cue that is identical, only a hint or clue close enough to allow your natural memory to kick in. It takes a bit of imagination, but again that can be fun.

3. **Write it.** Write the name along with its more memorable association, then next to it or below it write the quote, concept, or actions from the text that you want to remember was associated with this person. In this case we would have, "Drusilla Hendricks drew silly hen pics, as she waited to starve to death, but the Lord heard her prayers and sent others with food."

This technique can be used to remember the names of places you are unfamiliar with, like Quincy. One technique used above that may work is to think of something that rhymes with it, like, "The folks were not chintzy who lived in Quincy."

4. **Periodic rehearsal.** Practice rehearsing the name and connection at spaced intervals. You may want to keep a list of these hard-to-remember names; their reminder picture, person, or phrase; and the related text or concepts you want to remember. Periodically review your list.

Where Can That Be Found?

Recently an astute friend was telling me about a principle of forgiveness taught in the Doctrine and Covenants, and he wanted me to look it up, but he couldn't recall where it was. Has that ever happened to you? If you wanted someone to read up on the Lord's teachings regarding forgiveness, the oath and covenant of the priesthood, how to lead a family in righteousness, the formulas for obtaining the blessings of the Lord, or the abundance of the earth, would you know where to find them? (This is assuming you are familiar with these teachings and are not at your computer.)

In this section you will learn an easy system for recalling where important doctrines can be found and a system for remembering the chronology of important events in Church history, or when various doctrines were revealed. First, learn an easy, but ingenious system for associating numbers (section numbers or dates) with teachings or events.

This method is based on a system developed centuries ago for remembering numbers called the phonetic number system. This is based on several important principles we discussed in the last chapter, particularly the Relate and Concrete principles.

Since numbers are generally harder to envision and remember than concrete objects you can picture, symbolic systems have been devised to come up with other easily envisioned objects, people, or actions that can be used as symbols to represent numbers. Our entire language is a symbolic system that has been developed to enable us to use graphic or more visual symbols—lines, shapes, ink or dot patterns, and engravings—to represent mental concepts and ideas. The phonetic number system is an extension of that.

For example, a tie can be used to represent the number 1. After all it looks like a big, long 1. A five-point star (such as a sheriff might have) has been used to represent the number 5. A skeleton key has been used to represent the number 7, again because the appearance is similar. Say you were going shopping and had seven items you wanted to pick up. If you had learned a symbolic number system like this, you could easily recall these items by simply associating each with the symbol used to represent numbers 1 to 7.

Say the first item was a box of tissues. You might imagine a tie being wrapped or tied around the box. If the fifth item on your list was an avocado, you might imagine a star being pinned to the avocado. If your seventh item was a jar of peanut butter, you could imagine a large skeleton key sticking out of the top of the jar. Since each of these images is unusual or extraordinary, it's likely you would remember them.

As you enter to the store you could ask yourself, "What is the first item I need?" Knowing that a tie represents the number, you would ask, "What have I related to a tie?" and immediately you would recall the image of the tie wrapped around the box of tissue. Say you picked up items 2 to 4, but could not immediately recall what the next item was. All you would have to do is ask yourself, "Okay, this is item 5, the symbol for 5 is a star. What is my star stuck to?" and immediately an avocado would spring to mind. Then again for seven, as you thought of a key, you would remember the image of it being stuck in the top of a jar of peanut butter.

If any of these images is not memorable enough, all you would have to do is go back, and using the optimizing strategies learned in the last chapter, devise more memorable images. You might make them more exaggerated, like a flaming red six-foot-long tie wrapped around the box so tight the tissues are falling out, or maybe you have a bunch of boxes bundled with a tie. You could have a three-foot-tall glowing star stuck in a ten-pound avocado; or the key could be protruding through the side of the peanut butter jar, with the glass broken, and peanut butter dripping all over; or you could have a peanut butter jar shaped like a key. The possibilities are endless, and creating them can be a fun, as well as a good exercise for your imagination and your brain.

Where Is That Written?

Now that you understand the basic concept, let's move on to how to remember larger numbers, like section numbers in the Doctrine and Covenants, which we can then link to section content. This simple system can enable you to remember numbers 0 to 9, assuming you have a concrete, easily envisioned symbol to represent each number. But how about larger numbers like 1823?

In the seventeenth century Stanislaus Mink von Wennsshein came up with a phonetic number system. It was expanded by Dr. Richard Grey in 1730. Then William James, considered to be the father of psychology, included it in his *Principles of Psychology*, published in 1890. In this ingenious system, developed during the time of the Restoration, each number 0 to 9 was assigned a phonetic sound (as in Hebrew, these are all consonant sounds).

The number 1 was given a *t* or a *d* sound. Perhaps because the *t* looks like a 1, and the *d* could be seen as a pregnant 1. An *n* was used to represent 2. You will note it has 2 legs. An *m* sound represents 3. It has 3 legs. An *r* sound was chosen to represent 4; the fourth letter in the word *four* is an *r*. A 5 is represented by the *l* sound. Perhaps that was derived from the *L* in Roman numbers used to represent 500. The 6 was given the *j* or *sh* sound. You will note *j* looks like a backward 6. The 7 has the *k* sound. You can imagine a backward 7 leaning against the *I*. The *f* and related *v* sound was used for 8, perhaps because a cursive *f* looks like an 8. And the *p* or *b* sound was used to represent 9, since the *p* looks like a backward 9. The zero has a *z* sound as in zero, or an *s* sound. What follows are the numbers 0 to 9 with their corresponding phonetic sounds (read these as sounds rather than as letters).

0	1	2	3	4	5	6	7	8	9
s	t	n	m	r	L	sh	k	f	p
c	d					j	g	v	b
z						ch	c (hard)		

By saying each sound associated with each number you will soon pick up the associated sounds. If you run through them a few times you will find them easier to remember.

However, you don't even need to remember these sounds, so long as you can remember the picture words that go with each number. You see, from each of these sounds, easily pictured words were selected to represent each number. Each picture word or symbol contains only the consonant sounds associated with its corresponding number, like *tie* for 1, *Noah* for 2, *mow* for 3, *row* for 4, and so forth. In this system, the vowel sounds do not count, nor does an *h* or *w* sound, or an *o* at the beginning of the word. So for example this system uses Noah to represent 2, because the name starts with an *n* sound and the rest of the letters don't count or they are silent. Noah, of course was also the father of the second birth of the earth.

For most numbers there are several options that could be used. For example, to represent the number 12 you could use the words TiN, TeeN, ToNe, TuNe, TaN, DaN, DoNe, DuNe, DiNe, or DeN. For my purposes I usually use the word TiN—and picture a tin can. I've selected tin can because it is a concrete, familiar object, that can easily be linked with other objects with a little action, like a swift kick.

The original system consisted of a hundred picture words representing the numbers 1 to 100. Most modern memory performers or mnemonists use a variation of this system, as we will here. Many of the symbols or picture words have been changed or adapted to make them more concrete and contemporary, but the underlying phonetic numbering system has remained the same.

1. tie
2. Noah
3. mow (lawn mower)
4. row or oar
5. law man (sheriff)
6. shoe
7. key
8. sofa
9. pie
10. toes
11. tot (toddler) or toad
12. tin can (or cup)
13. tombstone
14. tire
15. towel
16. dish or tissue
17. tack or duck
18. TV
19. tub
20. noose or newspaper
21. net
22. nun
23. nameplate
24. winner (trophy)
25. nail
26. nudge
27. knock
28. knife (electric)
29. nap (hammock)
30. moss or moose
31. mitt (baseball mitt)
32. man (man in black)
33. mom
34. mirror or hammer
35. mail (mail carrier's bag)
36. match that lights and burns
37. microphone
38. movie
39. mop
40. rose
41. radio
42. horn (bugle)
43. Ram (truck)
44. rear (horse rearing up)
45. railroad track
46. rash (itching)
47. rake
48. roof
49. rope
50. lace (shoelace)
51. light (flashlight)
52. lion
53. limb or llama
54. lure (fishing hook)
55. lollipop
56. leech
57. lock or lick
58. loaf of bread
59. laptop computer
60. jazz (saxophone)
61. shot (with a needle)
62. shin (kick in the)
63. jam
64. chair
65. Jell-o
66. judge (gavel)
67. shock
68. shave (as with a razor)
69. jeep
70. gauze
71. kite
72. cane
73. comb
74. crow
75. coal
76. cage
77. gag
78. coffee
79. cape
80. fuse
81. photo (snapping a photo)
82. fan
83. foam
84. fur
85. foil (wrapped in tin foil)
86. effigy (hung on a rope)
87. fig or fog
88. five
89. VIP
90. pizza
91. bat
92. piano
93. bomb
94. buy
95. bell
96. pitch (pitch a softball)
97. pack (back pack)
98. pave (as in pave the road)
99. pipe
100. daisies

I suggest you spend the next week practicing these. Go over them on a regular basis to keep them fresh in your memory, at least until you've used them all a number of times. After that they are easy to remember. But if you ever forget, just sound out the sounds representing the number you want and the picture word will be there waiting for you.

Let's apply this to remembering section numbers in the Doctrine and Covenants. To illustrate, I will use two topics noted at the beginning of this section. You will recall my friend wanted me to read what the Lord had said about forgiveness, specifically how often we should forgive. This is recorded in section 98. The symbol for 98 is "PaVe." In order to create a memorable picture relating the concept (forgiving) with the section it's in (98), I first need to anchor it, either to a place in the present or to the setting in which it was given. If I want to anchor it to something I am familiar with here and now, I might imagine that while I am paving my driveway with cement, my neighbor comes over and steps in it, not just once, but twice. Then I imagine a friend asking, "So how many times are you going to forgive him for doing that?"

If I were to put this into historical perspective, I might imagine one of the Saints in Missouri on his knees paving his driveway, when a member of the mob comes along and kicks (smites) him into the wet cement. I see the Saint rise covered in cement and hear him cry to the Lord, "How many times must I forgive this cruel injustice?" Then Joseph appears with the Lord's reply and doctrine on this subject.

Now, I know the Saints didn't pave their driveways with cement, and such is not mentioned in the Doctrine and Covenants. This is an image or symbol I've woven into the story to help me remember that the Lord teaches the doctrine of forgiveness in section 98 (PaVe).

The oath and covenant of the priesthood is discussed in section 84 (FuR). If I wanted to remember that in context I might imagine a meeting of three elders in Kirtland, joined by three more who are newly returned missionaries. Joseph is dressed in white robes of the priesthood, with a large brown fur collar. In this meeting he prophesies about the gathering of the Saints and the building of a temple. I imagine him lifting up a white fur-covered tote with a gold inscription that says, "Oath and Covenant of the Priesthood." The white robes remind me of the priesthood, and the fur, which I know is not in the text, reminds me that this revelation on the priesthood is in section 84 (FuR).

For Sections over 100

You can see how this system can help you to remember the location of any teaching in the first hundred sections of the Doctrine and Covenants, but how about the last thirty-eight? There are at least two ways you can approach this. First you can try to come up with thirty-eight new picture words that begin with the *t* or *d* sound and contain the other sounds representing the numbers 0 to 38.[4] However, I found it difficult to find good symbols to match all of these, plus the challenge of learning thirty-eight additional symbols.

So what I do is simply to add daisies (the symbol for 100) as I picture each word for numbers 1 to 38. For 101 I see daisies tied to a tie, for 102 Noah holding daisies, and for 113 daisies spouting up through a tombstone. For most of these revelations, I know they came later in Church history. For section 109, for example, I imagine pie being served and eaten at the dedication of the Kirtland temple, which I know was much later in Church history than section 9, which was given during the translation of the Book of Mormon. If I can remember to add a few daisies to that Kirtland pie, I will know it is section 109 and not section 9. This method seems to work quite well for me, and saves me from having to learn thirty-eight new symbols.

Remembering Verses

In previous books I have not encouraged readers to use this system to remember verses, but rather to envision and link the concepts in order within a chapter, and then remember where the concepts fall, whether they are in the opening, center, or end of the chapter. Usually that is sufficient for most chapters, people, and purposes.

Trying to tie every concept to every verse is too tedious and will introduce too many foreign objects into the text. However, the Doctrine and Covenants does have some very long sections covering many different topics. So it seems appropriate to add another simple numbering system to break this down a bit further to assist those desiring to remember both section and related verses.

Rhyming Symbols Numbering Systems

Since this need to recall the location of important text is as old as books, it's no wonder there have been several systems developed to help people remember numbers in general, and chapter, page, or verse numbers in particular. One of the easiest of such systems to learn and use is the rhyming system. This system has paired words that rhyme with each number. One form is as follows.

zero: hero
one: bun
two: glue
three: tree
four: door
five: hive
six: sticks
seven: heaven (a harp)
eight: gate
nine: dine
ten: hen

Typically this system is used to remember numbered items within a text, especially when the items number ten or fewer, as with the ten commandments. It could also be used with an adaptation (as noted above for numbers over a hundred) to remember the thirteen Articles of Faith in or out of order.[3] For the Doctrine and Covenants I use it to help me remember groups of verses. Most concepts or teachings take more than one or two verses to explain. So rather than trying to tie concepts to specific verses, I usually tie them to groups of ten as follows.

Hero: verses 0–10
Bun: verses 11–19
Glue: verses 20–29
Tree: verses 30–39
Door: verses 40–49
Beehive: verses 50–59
Sticks: verses 60–69
Heaven (harp): verses 70–79
Gate: verses 80–89
Dine: verses 90–99

If the verses I want to recall start between 0 and 10, I imagine one of my heroes—Christ or Joseph Smith—in the opening scene. For 11 to 19 a bun will be there somewhere, and for 20 to 29 things will be glued or sticky, and so forth up to 99.

For verses between 100 and 110 I use a hen. There are four sections in the Doctrine and Covenants with more than 110 verses. So for those verses greater than 110, I imagine a hen plus the next numerical object. For 111 to 119 I imagine the hen with a hamburger bun draped over her back, for 120 to 129 she is stuck to things with glue, for 130 to 139 she's up in a tree, laying eggs that fall on the subject matter with yolk-colored splatter. And for verses over 140 (in sections 88 and 124) I imagine the hen with a small door hung around her neck.

Hen: verses 100–109
Hen and bun: verses 110–119
Hen and glue: verses 120–129
Hen in tree: verses 130–139
Hen and door: verses 140–145

If it is important to you to give a specific chapter and verse, there are at least two ways of doing this. The first is to use one phonetic number symbol to remember the section, as noted above, and another phonetic symbol to remember the verse. But if you do this I suggest you make the verse symbol much smaller when you picture these together, or in different colors, say red for section symbols and bright green for verse symbols.

For example, say you want to remember the specific reference for D&C 121:41, "No power or influence can or ought to be maintained by virtue of the priesthood, only by persuasion, by long-suffering, by gentleness and meekness, and by love unfeigned."

The symbol for 121 would be a net with daisies, the symbol for 41, a radio. So you might imagine a father (or perhaps yourself) with a red fishing net draped over his shoulders, with daisies poking out, who is trying to influence his son to, let's say, listen to uplifting music instead of urban jungle rap. In an effort to persuade him, the father has one arm gently around his son's shoulder as a gesture of love, and in his other hand he holds a small green radio, which only plays uplifting music. He tells his son they have all suffered this jungle rap long enough and he now offers this tiny green radio as an incentive for change.

You could also add the particular verse to the system noted above. In this case you would have the father with the net and daisies, and a door in the scene (representing verses 40 to 49). Imagine that as the father talks with his son, he points to a tie hanging on a nearby door, which the father then offers to the son in an effort to persuade him.

I prefer this method, although I use it sparingly. Generally verses should be read in context anyway. Narrowing a location down to within ten verses is usually specific enough for me and leaves less clutter.

Remembering Church History

Concepts or teachings are generally best remembered in context. Therefore, as you learn the doctrines of the Doctrine and Covenants, it's best if you can learn and remember the history and chronology of events as you go. Section 8, for example, makes better sense if you understand it was given to Oliver Cowdery during the time that he was helping to translate the Book of Mormon. Section 121 is best understood in the context of Joseph's suffering in Liberty Jail while the Saints suffered cruel persecution at the hands of mobsters in Missouri.

In this section there are a few additional principles and ideas for remembering the sequence of events associated with Church history and the Doctrine and Covenants.

First, it helps if you can develop and affix in your mind a clear mental map of where various events occurred. This provides a framework for anchoring or tying down other memories and greatly helps in memory organization and recall. This is one reason why our scriptures and manuals contain maps. Reviewing and studying these maps is a good way to begin to develop our own memory maps and anchors memories to a visual framework.

To help fill in this framework, watch movies that show these locations and depict the various events that occurred there. Movies like *Legacy*, *Emma Smith: My Story*, and other Church history vignettes all help to better envision what it was like. When I think of events in Church history, what pops into my mind is often a scene from a Church movie I've seen.

Perhaps one of the best aids to memory mapping, though not practical for everyone, is actually visiting these sites. A few years ago I helped my son move from Boston to Houston, and in the process we stopped by the old Smith farm near Palmyra, New York, where we saw the home where Joseph lived; walked through the Sacred Grove; and climbed the Hill Cumorah. Then we traveled to Kirtland, Ohio, where we took a tour of the Kirtland Temple, and saw the Melchizedek Priesthood pulpits where the Lord and later Moses, Elias, and Elijah appeared to Joseph and Oliver. From there we traveled to Nauvoo. Here I walked some of the same streets my ancestors once walked. The next morning we stopped by Carthage Jail. On another occasion I visited Independence, Missouri, and Liberty Jail.

Though not essential, these visits did help me to get a clearer picture of the setting for the events that had occurred there. However, whether you have been to these places, you cannot tell how they looked exactly back then, and so must of necessity use your imagination in this process of mental mapping. Nevertheless, maps, movies, pictures, and any other visual aids can help to create a memorable framework to fit your memories into.

Second, once you have the settings in mind, it's helpful if you can put events into chronological order using a natural linking procedure, as well as dates. I call this "natural linking" because it requires one to imagine the natural sequence of events as they actually occurred, such as when the Church moved from upstate New York to Ohio, and then many of the Saints moved to Missouri, while others remained in Ohio. After being driven from Missouri, they settled in Nauvoo, and then moved on to Utah. Using the maps at the end of the Doctrine and Covenants can also help in picturing the sequences of this tremendous migration and corresponding events in Church history.

However, the best way to anchor these events in your mind is to read Gerald N. Lund's series *The Work and the Glory*. Lund brings these people and events back to life, and you obtain a comprehensive and accurate understanding of Church history. If you are short on time, the movie series by the same title can also help, although it's not nearly as rich in detail.

When Did That Happen?

The other thing that can help is remembering dates, and you already know how to do that. It's just a matter of remembering a few more numbers. Don't be dismayed by the magnitude of the numbers like 1847. Most of the prominent events in Church history occurred in the early 1800s; in fact, 90 percent occurred within just an eighteen-year period between 1827 and 1845.

In order to remember what happened when, all you have to do is link those dates, using the phonetic number system, with the events that occurred during that time period. If you want be more specific to remember events month by month, the numeric rhyming system can be used to remember the months 1 to 10

(January to October) with a turkey thrown in to represent events during the month of November, and sleigh bells to represent December events.

Specific days can also be remembered. Use the phonetic system and visualize these symbols in purple or some other color.

So for example, if you wanted to remember when the first missionary, Samuel Smith, was sent out, you would think of the phonetic symbol for 30 (for the year 1830), a moose, and the rhyming symbol for 6 (for June), sticks, and tie those to Samuel's leaving on a mission. Perhaps you would envision Joseph in Fayette, New York, setting apart someone you know named Sam to preach the gospel. You envision him climbing on a moose with a bag of copies of the Book of Mormon dangling from sticks he has slung over his shoulder to ride off to do missionary work.

In fact, that moose gets involved in a lot of things that year, including the organization of the Church. Following the Chinese tradition, we could call that the year of the moose. If you need some help getting your brain into this type of imagery you might try reading the children's book *If You Give a Moose a Muffin*. Of course there is no record of a moose in Fayette, and Samuel certainly didn't ride off on one. We know that's just inserted into the picture to help us remember events that occurred in 1830.

If you want to be more specific and remember, for example, the exact date when the temple site in Independence was dedicated, you would think of the phonetic symbol for 31 (for the year 1831), mitt; the rhyming symbol for 8 (August), gate; and then throw in a little purple lawn mower for 3, the actual date of dedication. You might imagine the Prophet and others in a grassy meadow in Missouri. You are there with your lawn mower. Joseph calls and others to come and help lift the rock into place for the dedication of the temple. One brother with a large mitt on lifts one sharp corner while they slide an old gate under it. Then they lift it onto your lawn mower to move it into place.

That's not too bad. The challenge comes when you want to remember the exact date an event occurred that is mentioned in the Doctrine and Covenants, and you also want to recall the specific section and verse where that event is recorded. Fortunately there are not a lot of those. But there are several. One example would be remembering the date Elijah appeared in the Kirtland Temple, and the section and verse it is recorded in the Doctrine and Covenants. Using this system would require introducing five artificial symbols into the picture. While it is possible, it could make the scene cluttered and confusing. If you can just recall where the event is mentioned in the Doctrine and Covenants, that will usually have the specific dates. Or you can just rely on natural memory with no artificial symbols to remember one or the other. For this I would think it easiest to remember that this event occurred on April 3, 1836, shortly after the Kirtland Temple was dedicated and three days before the Savior's birth date—the day Elijah was prophesied to come.

To recall the section where this is recorded you may imagine that all of those who appeared on that occasion as noted in the Doctrine and Covenants had daisies sprouting up between their toes, signifying that these events were recorded in section 110. As Elijah approaches, he stubs his toe on a tombstone and notes there was none such for him, because he did not die. But we know the tombstone is only there to remind us that His coming is recorded in verse 13 of section 110.

If you really want to remember both—when events occurred, and where they are recorded in the Doctrine and Covenants—start with the most important historical dates first, since they are easier to put in place and fewer in number (see Appendix B). Once you have those down, you can picture and link the symbols for each section number to the teachings and events in each section. Otherwise, it could become confusing. On the other hand, learning all of that would make for a fun mental challenge!

The easy way to remember this is to remember that Elijah appeared on the same day the Savior appeared to Joseph and

Oliver in the Kirtland temple, which was in the year the Kirtland temple was dedicated, 1836, and three days prior to the Savior's birth date (April 6). So this occurred on April 3, 1836. But if you were just using the phonetic number system, you would link a match, the symbol for 36, with this temple Pentecostal period. You could imagine that angels with matches made the temple appear as if it were on fire. And Elijah, the Lord, and others all enter through a large white cosmic door (April) followed by a tiny bright, yellow lawn mower.

6

A WORD OF WISDOM

"Warned and forewarned . . . and treasures of knowledge"
—D&C 89:4, 19

One of the plagues now sweeping the land relevant to remembering is Alzheimer's disease and similar dementias.[1] There are more than 5.2 million people in the United States now suffering from these memory disorders, and that number is expected to double in the next twenty years as the baby boomers age. Advancing age, however, is not the only or even the primary cause of this growing number. Elderly people in other parts of the world, such as China, Japan, India, and even some parts of Africa and Italy, have significantly fewer incidents of these disorders than those in the United States.[2] Moreover, doctors in America are seeing "an alarming increase" in early onset cases of dementia, with individuals in their thirties and forties now developing these problems.[3] So if age isn't the primary cause of this increase, what is?

Researchers have been puzzling over the causes of dementia for decades, but especially in recent years as the numbers have increased. While scientists have not yet found a cure, we now know much more about what contributes to these ailments and how to reduce our risk. We may even know enough to arrest or reverse these disorders if caught in the early stages.

Currently I teach the Maintain Your Brain™ course for the Utah Chapter of the Alzheimer's Association. In conjunction with this, I write a monthly review of new related research, so I am constantly being updated on the latest greatest studies in this ongoing drive for a cure. What we now know is that in addition to genetic factors (which account for only about 30 percent of cases)[4] various other common ailments and injuries increase one's risk as well. These include:

- High blood pressure
- High blood sugar—diabetes
- High cholesterol or cardiovascular disease
- Obesity
- Depression or high prolonged stress
- Head trauma or injuries
- Metabolic syndrome
- Sleep apnea or prolonged lack of sleep
- Addiction to cigarettes[5]

With current trends, the average baby boomer has about a one in eight chance of developing Alzheimer's before age eighty,[6] and about a 50 percent chance thereafter, if something isn't done to prevent it. However, studies show that if you have any of the condition during midlife your risk goes up significantly. If you have two of these it may double; three or more it will more than quadruple.[7] In other words, such a person will have better than a fifty-fifty chance of developing dementia before age eighty if other significant changes do not occur.

How are Latter-day Saints doing? We've prided ourselves in living a healthy lifestyle because we obey the Word of Wisdom. In the 1970s studies showed Latter-day Saints tended to live longer, with lower rates of cancer and other diseases. How about now? In June 2006, Brigham Young University reported LDS people living in Utah are 14 percent more likely to be obese than those of other faiths; in 1996 it was 34 percent.[8] This has caused no small concern, because it is well known that obesity is a major risk factor for high blood pressure, diabetes, heart disease, depression, sleep apnea, and dementia.

How is Utah doing in regard to dementia? Currently we are second in the nation in expected new cases per capita. It saddens my heart as I travel around Utah and see so many good Saints and their families suffering from this devastating disease.

Yet in all fairness, it should be noted that one of the reasons for this is because of living the Word of Wisdom, LDS seniors tend to live longer. As we live longer our risk for developing dementia increases. But this is of little consolation to the thirty-five thousand individuals and their families who suffer from this frustrating and debilitating ailment in Utah. How do we prevent this? How do we reduce this robber of memories? If you or a loved one has already started to develop memory problems, is there anything you can do now to arrest this robber of memories? Fortunately, there is.

There is a fear, however, among a growing number that we have come to rely too much upon modern medicine to keep us healthy. We've become accustomed to living as we would like to live and then when we are ill we run to the doctor who should be able to "fix us up." We've come to expect some miracle drug to bail us out, repair the damage, and keep us going. But that's not a healthy model, and some believe it will never happen with Alzheimer's because there are too many factors involved.

A Solution to the Health Care Crisis in America

What do you notice about the list of health risk factors in the last section? Do the items have anything in common? As I reviewed this and related studies some months ago while preparing for a radio program in Salt Lake City, it dawned on me that all of these problems, except for genetics and head trauma, were related to one thing, something that the Lord had already counseled us on—our diet and what we allow into our bodies.

A review of eighteen studies conducted in eleven countries caught my attention. In this study they noted that those who ate less calories, less animal fat, and more antioxidants and trace minerals from plant sources had only one-third the rate of dementia as average Americans, including their relatives living in the United States.[9]

To reinforce that age, ethnicity, or genetics are not the primary drivers here, another study in New York showed that those who followed the Mediterranean diet were 60 percent less likely to develop Alzheimer's than their neighbors who did not.[10]

What were the dietary differences that accounted for this variation? A closer analysis showed that what the rural Asian, African, and Mediterranean diets had in common were far more vegetables, fruits, and fish; and far less other meat, trans fats, salt, and processed foods that are common in the typical American diet. More recent studies in France and Japan have shown similar results: those whose ate less green and yellow vegetables, fruits, fish, and other kinds of meat had significantly higher levels of Alzheimer's or other dementia.[11]

The unhealthy diet in America has not always been this way. On the website www.originalfastfoods.com, Word of Wisdom advocates James and Colleen Simmons cite a U.S. Department of Agriculture study documenting some of the changes that have occurred in the U.S. diet in the last century.[12] They include:

Animal-based foods: average consumption has more

than doubled from less than 20 percent of caloric intake to 42 percent.

Fat: consumption has more than doubled.

Sugar: has more than doubled.

Cheese: is seven times greater.

Soda pop: is seven times greater.

Salad oil: is more than thirteen times greater.

Fresh garden produce: reduced more than thirteen times.

Grain: consumption reduced by a hundred pounds per person per year, and shifted from whole grains to mostly refined and processed grain products.

Could this be one reason why we are having a health care crisis in this country? In 1979 President Ezra Taft Benson, the former U.S. Secretary of Agriculture and one of the most knowledgeable authorities the Church has ever had on food, nutrition, and the Word of Wisdom, noted: "To a significant degree we are an overfed and undernourished nation digging an early grave with our teeth, and lacking the energy that could be ours because we overindulge in junk foods."[13]

What to Do

We know the "don'ts" of the Word of Wisdom, but what about the "do's"? The Lord directed Joseph Smith in terms of what we should be eating.

> And again, verily I say unto you, all wholesome herbs God hath ordained for the constitution, nature, and use of man—
>
> Every herb in the season thereof, and every fruit in the season thereof; all these to be used with prudence and thanksgiving.
>
> Yea, flesh also of beasts and of the fowls of the air, I, the Lord, have ordained for the use of man with thanksgiving; nevertheless they are to be used sparingly;
>
> And it is pleasing unto me that they should not be used, only in times of winter, or of cold, or famine.
>
> All grain is ordained for the use of man and of beasts, to be the staff of life, not only for man but for the beasts of the

> field, and the fowls of heaven, and all wild animals that run or creep on the earth;
>
> And these hath God made for the use of man only in times of famine and excess of hunger.
>
> All grain is good for the food of man; as also the fruit of the vine; that which yieldeth fruit, whether in the ground or above the ground. (D&C 89:10–16)

In the mentioned health studies, meat was kept to a minimum, except perhaps for fish. However, here the Lord says He has ordained the flesh of beasts and fowl, "for the use of man" (v. 12). That's what most of us remember, but if we look below, He adds, "they are to be used sparingly; And it is pleasing unto me that they *should not be used*, only in times of winter, or of cold, or famine" (vv. 12–13, emphasis added). Do we as Latter-day Saints really abide by this part of the Word of Wisdom?

Recent diabetic research suggests that it's beneficial to not cook meat too fast at too high of heat, as in frying, broiling, roasting, and grilling. Healthier preparations include boiling, braising, marinating, poaching, steaming, or stewing in a crock pot with water and seasonings, like lemon juice, broth, olive oil, or cider vinegar. The browning from broiling or even toasting causes glycotoxins, especially in fat and protein, which lead to inflammation, oxidation, free radical damage, and aging. The vitamin B-1 may help prevent that, but such practices are best avoided.[14]

I was raised on a dairy farm, with pigs, chickens, cows, horses, and goats, and growing up I loved to eat all of them—except the horses. I just rode those to round up the rest. I love bacon. (You will note the present tense.) I love pot roast, fried chicken, pork ribs, and mutton, and especially the warm, fatty, greasy parts. I love French fries and onion rings deep fried in fat. But I rarely eat them any more, especially in warm weather. Why? Four reasons: It appears to me the Lord is saying it would please Him if I did not use these in the warmer months. Second, I've found the relevant research suggests they are not optimal for my health. In fact, I know they can affect my thinking ability and memory. Third, recently I had a scan of my carotid arteries and they found focal plaque—not good. And finally, recalling Dr. Morrow's statement from chapter 2, they may even have an adverse impact on my ability to learn and receive revelation (see D&C 89:19).

So What's a Guy to Eat Anyway?

Regarding the Word of Wisdom President Benson noted, "What needs additional emphasis are the positive aspects—*the need for more vegetables, fruits and grains.*"[15] I found when my diet was full of meat I didn't realize the alternatives, or how good they could be, even though I thought I ate a healthy diet. But the Lord was quite clear as to what we could eat. Section 89's footnote 10a, for "herbs," says, "plants." In other words the Lord is saying He has ordained "all wholesome *plants* . . . for the constitution, nature, and use of man." Additional references make that even clearer. Genesis 1:29 says, "God said, Behold, I have given you every herb bearing seed, which is upon the face of all the earth, and every tree, in the which is the fruit of a tree yielding seed; to you it shall be for meat."

What should the main course of our diet be? It's clear that it's to be plants—primarily vegetable, fruit, grains, beans, nuts, seeds, herbs, and so forth. That's exactly what the experts say the research shows is best for our body and brain.

One of the worst things for our vascular system and brain is high levels of homocysteine.[16] This is an amino acid associated with inflammation. Too much can damage the hippocampus, the memory center of the brain. Homocysteine is also involved in the formation of the amyloid plaque that is characteristic of Alzheimer's disease. However, scientists have found that two basic B-vitamins can dramatically reduce levels of homocysteine, cutting one's risk for Alzheimer's nearly in half.[17] These vitamins, folate or folic acid and vitamin B-12, come from leafy green vegetables. Folate comes from spinach, mustard greens, cowpeas, chickpeas, lentils, kidney beans, navy beans, and fresh orange juice. Sources of vitamin B-12 include meat, fish, eggs, and skim milk. However, we don't need much of this vitamin, and the body can usually store it for weeks at a time.

The other B-vitamins are essential for the brain and nervous system and are necessary to help break down foods and build the neurotransmitters of attention and memory. They can be found in potatoes, bananas, lentils, chili peppers, tuna, brewer's yeast, and molasses, and most whole grain products.

Most refined grains have been milled, a process that removes the bran and germ. This is done to give grains a finer texture and improve their shelf life, but it also removes dietary fiber, iron, and many B-vitamins. So whole grain products tend to be best, so long as they do not have too much added sugar. In addition to contributing to diabetes, refined sugar can deplete these valuable B-vitamins from the body and brain.

President Benson said, "In general, the more food we eat in its *natural* state and the *less it is refined without additives*, the healthier it will be for us. Food can affect the mind, and deficiencies in certain elements in the body can promote mental depression."[18]

Additionally, there is some evidence to suggest that the minerals in vegetables, particularly green and yellow ones, helps remove various toxins from our system, like mercury, aluminum, lead, heated plastics, and sodium fluoride that are present in increasing quantities in our food and environment. Other toxins are produced as a natural by-product of energy production, and tend to cause inflammation and damage to the sensitive cell membranes and DNA in our bodies and brains. Vegetables and fruit help prevent that.

Eat More Antioxidants

In the internationally famous Cache County Study on Memory, Health and Aging conducted by Utah State University, researchers found those who had the highest amounts of vitamins C and E in their diets had the lowest risk for developing dementia.[19] This emphasizes the importance of antioxidants such as vitamins C and E in our diets, to arrest and quench the neurologically damaging effects of free radicals in our bodies, which are a natural result of eating, thinking, breathing, and exercise.

More powerful antioxidants have now been found. In a recent study published in the June 2008 issue of the *Journal of Neuroscience*, researchers found that the substance in the seeds and skins of dark colored grapes and raisins prevented the build-up of amyloid plaque in the brain cells of mice.[20] Similar antioxidant compounds are available in some other fruits and vegetables as well. The most potent antioxidants are in bright red and dark purple fruits and berries. The red annatto bean from Central America is the source of perhaps the most powerful type of vitamin E, tocotrienols. Almonds and wheat germ are other good sources. Vitamin C and related compounds are found in tomatoes, potatoes, and melons, cherries, berries, kiwi, and citrus fruits. Other powerful antioxidants found to help the brain are in blueberries, blackberries, wolfberries (also known as goji berries), the Açai berry, black currants, guava, mangos, papaya, and nearly every other type of fruit.

President Benson encouraged the Saints to eat a variety of foods, particularly vegetables, fruits, and grains. More recent guidelines suggest seven to thirteen servings per day, noting your choices should contain a wide variety of colors. They call this the "rainbow diet." This is one of the best ways we can insure we are getting enough of the nutrients our body and brain need to function well.

Fats and Brain Fitness

In the classes and seminars I teach I like to ask people what the brain and its billions of cells are made of. Is it primarily protein, carbohydrates, fats, minerals (rocks), or what? Many don't realize the brain is made up mostly of fats or lipids, and it is in a constant state of repair and rebuilding itself. Therefore, it is crucial for the health of our brain and memory that we consume adequate amounts of good fats, particularly those found in the omega-3 fatty acids and lecithin. These good fats also can be found in a variety of plant sources including flax seeds, chia seeds, algae, walnuts, canola oil, wheat germ, soy beans, spinach, pursland, summer squash, sesame seeds, avacados, almonds, strawberries, blueberries, bananas, sweet potatoes, and apple peels.

The most essential of these fatty acids, however, are no longer plentiful in our food chain. The fatty acid docosahexaenoic acid (DHA) is critical for the brain growth of infants. The best source is a mother's milk. Low DHA has been linked to violent behavior, ADHD, and other learning disorders, depression, and visual problems in children, as well as adults.[21] One study showed the IQs of breast-fed babies was eight points higher than those fed on infant formulas.[22] For that reason most formulas now contain added amounts of DHA, although it may not be as readily absorbed as from a mother's milk.

DHA also was once present in the meat of animals and game that grazed on grass lands. But now that most beef and chickens are fattened up in feedlots on corn and other grains, they no longer contain high amounts of DHA. One source remains readily available—coldwater fish. You may have heard that salmon and some other fish are good food for the brain, and that is true.

In one Chicago study, researchers found those who ate two or more pieces of fish per week, especially fish high in DHA, had 60 percent fewer cases of Alzheimer's and other dementia than those who ate fewer than one piece per week.[23] DHA is a potent neuro protector and has been shown to prevent and perhaps even reduce the amyloid plaque of Alzheimer's.[24]

An omega-3 fatty acid called linolenic acid can be converted by a young, healthy human body from other plant sources into DHA, but as the body ages it loses this ability. And much of our fish these days is polluted with mercury and other toxins. Therefore, fish oil, or DHA supplements (usually from algae sources) is often recommended in order to get the essential fats linolenic acids contain. There are some eggs now that are higher in DHA as well. Among fish, wild salmon, haddock, and light tuna in water seem to be among the safest sources. Small fish like sardines and krill are said to be safer. It's significant in the Word of Wisdom that fish or things that swim are not noted as being displeasing to the Lord for us to eat in any season (see D&C 89:12–13).

However, if the body cannot obtain enough essential or polyunsaturated fats from linolenic acid, it will resort to whatever it can find. Monounsaturated from olive oil is believed to be the next best, and saturated fats are okay in small amounts. Pure virgin coconut oil may be good for the brain. But fried fats, trans fats such as hydrogenated and partially hydrogenated fats, and oils typically used in processed baked goods (which may also contain aluminum), frozen waffles, margarine, and all fried food are a disaster for the brain. The brain will try to use them, but these fats make rigid, tough, sluggish brain cells that are more susceptible to oxidation and disease. One of the leading neurologists in the United States in this area, Dr. David Perlmutter, says, "A brain filled with trans-fatty acids is going to age faster and become progressively less functional. These fats are also linked to an increased risk of diabetes, and heart disease, two ailments associated with an increased risk of dementia and depression."[19]

He adds this caution: "Perhaps the most dangerous aspect of trans-fatty acids is that they crowd out healthier fats. Even if you eat lots of good fat along with trans-fatty and take an essential fatty acid supplement, the trans-fatty acids are the ones that will end up in your cell membranes."[20]

Many other preservatives and sweeteners like high-fructose corn syrup are hard for the body to handle as well and may contribute to diabetes, neurological problems, and other health problems.

The Solution

Obey the Word of Wisdom. It's apparent that like the rural Asian, African, or Mediterranean peoples, we would be wise to eat primarily a plant-based diet, whole fresh fruit, vegetables, nuts, grains, beans, and seeds generally unrefined as God prepared them, "in the season thereof" (D&C 89:11). We should also eat some fish, and other meat *sparingly* in winter months, rather than relying on the designs of conspiring men who want to make a buck by altering these foods. Seldom are altered foods as nutritionally enhancing as are whole foods mentioned in the Word of Wisdom for the body and brain. God knew how it would be, and so we have been "warned and forewarned" (D&C 84:4).

If we add to this a bit of good old-fashioned physical exercise (at least thirty minutes a day) to get these good nutrients circulated to our brain—after all the Word of Wisdom does note that if we eat right we should then be able "walk and not faint" (D&C 89:20)—we are promised that we may then find "treasures of knowledge, even hidden treasures" (v. 19) if we seek them.

Additional information on this topic including recipes, other healthy foods, and a few plant-based food supplements that have proven to be beneficial for the brain and memory can be found at www.ARECORD4LDS.com, as well as at www.originalfastfoods.com—one of my favorite sites for Word of Wisdom insights and ideas for natural healthy ways to lose fat and gain overall health.

NOTES

1. Dementia refers to a variety of disorders affecting cognitive ability, especially memory problems. Alzheimer's disease is the most common cause of dementia. There are at least twenty other causes. Vascular dementia is the second most common type.

2. For a good review, see *The China Study*, by T. Colin and Thomas M. Campbell (Dallas, TX: Benbella Books, 2006), 218–220.

3. Personal communication with Kathy Moran from the Center for Alzheimer's Care Imaging and Research at the University of Utah Medical Center, April 18, 2008.

4. Carla K. Johnson, "Kids Fear 2 Parents With Alzheimer's," ABC News, 10 March 2008. http://abcnews.go.com/Health/MindMoodNews/wireStory?id=4423128.

5. Alzheimer's Association, "Maintain Your Brain, How to Live a Brain Healthy Lifestyle," Participants Workbook, 2006, and Alzheimer's Disease, "Risk Factors." www.alz.org/alzheimers_disease_causes_risk_factors.asp#riskfactors.

6. Alzheimer's Association, *2008 Alzheimer's Disease Facts and Figures*, 34. Accessed from www.alz.org.

7. Miia Kivipelto; Anttila, Tiia, et al. "Body Mass Index, Clustering, of vascular risk factors, and the risk of dementia: A longitudinal, population-based study." *Neurobiology of Aging*, July 2004, Vol. 25 S2, p. S311. This study found that those who had high blood pressure, high cholesterol, and obesity were six times more likely to develop dementia.

8. Andrew, Little. "Spiritually fit but not physically fit." *Scroll Online: Brigham Young University—Idaho*. 7 June 2006, www.byui.edu/Scroll/archive/20060606/news3.html.

   See also "Are Latter-day Saints Getting Fatter?" a great article about the Word of Wisdom and weight loss, available at www.meridianmagazine.com/healthyoutlook/080605fat.html.

9. William B. Grant. "Dietary Links to Alzheimer's Disease." Alzheimer's Disease Review 2, 1997, 42–55.

10. Nicholas Scarmeas, et al. "Mediterranean Diet, Alzheimer's Disease, and Vascular Mediation." *Archives of Neurology*, 2006; 63:1709-1717.

11. Dr. Otsuka, in the department of Neurology, Jichi Medical School, Omiya Medical Center in Japan, in a study involving sixty-four Alzheimer's patients.

12. Cited from "Major Trends in U.S. Food Supply, 1909–99," *Food Review*, Vol. 23, Iss. 1. Available at www.ers.usda.gov/publications/foodreview/jan2000/frjan2000b.pdf.

13. Ezra Taft Benson, "In His Steps," *1979 Devotional Speeches of the Year* (Provo, Utah: BYU, 1980), 62.

14. Steven V. Joyal, *What Your Doctor May Not Tell You About Diabetes* (FL: Life Extension Publications, 2008).

15. Ezra Taft Benson, "In His Steps," 62.

16. S. Seshadri et al., "Plasma homocysteine as a risk factor for dementia and Alzheimer's disease," *New England Journal of Medicine*, 2002; 346(7):476–483. Available at http://lpi.

oregonstate.edu/infocenter/vitamins/vitaminB12/b12refs.html#ref16.

17. Linus Pauling Institute, Oregon State University, "Micronutrients Information Center," http://lpi.oregonstate.edu/infocenter/vitamins/vitaminB12/b12refs.html#ref16.

18. Ezra Taft Benson, "Do Not Despair," *Ensign*, Nov. 1974, 65. Emphasis added.

19. Peter P. Zandi, et al, "Reduced Risk of Alzheimer's Disease in Users of Antioxidant Vitamin Supplements: The Cache County Study," *Archives of Neurology* 2004, 61:82–88.

20. Giulio Pasinetti, *"Animal study indicates grape seed extract may reduce cognitive decline associated with Alzheimer's disease,"* SfN News Releases, *17 June 2008.* www.sfn.org/?pagename=news_061708b.

21. David Perlmutter, *The Better Brain Book*, 112.

22. Ibid.

23. Morris, Martha Clare et al. "Fish consumption and cognitive decline with age in a large community study." *Archives of Neurology* 2005; 62(12):1849–53.

24. Mosakowski Tom, "The Omega-3 Fatty Acid DHA Confirmed to Deter Alzheimer's," Natural News.com, 15 February, 2008, http://www.naturalnews.com/022649.html

25. Perlmutter, *The Better Brain Book*, 65.

26. Ibid.

7

PULLING IT ALL TOGETHER

"Organize yourselves; prepare every needful thing"
—D&C 109: 8

So far you have learned a variety of methods, strategies, tools, and techniques to help you remember the teachings of the Doctrine and Covenants and Church history. Now let's discuss a more comprehensive plan for pulling it all together into one cohesive master strategy. I've worked with enough students to know that what works for one person may not work well for another. The techniques that I think are great may not be so great for you, because each of us is different in learning styles. On the other hand, it is of considerable value to see how others do things. Here are some things that I and others have done in helping us remember the scriptures and Church history.

I hope you will create some better procedures than we have. When you do, please share them on the website at www.ARECORD4LDS.com. That's part of the gospel's plan, to "instruct and edify each other" (D&C 43:8) for our mutual benefit and progression.

It's helpful to start by getting the big picture. This is the first step in the popular SQ4R study skills method taught at most major universities. The letters SQ4R stand for Survey, Question, Read, wRite, Recite, and Review. Studies that led to the development of SQ4R showed that people retained more of their reading if they first did a quick survey of the material to get the main idea, and then formulated a few questions to ask themselves as they read the material. Then they would read it to find the answers to their questions, write down their answers, practice reciting the answers, and then review what they had learned.

Now you may not always have time to use this approach. It may not seem practical for a casual reading of the Doctrine and Covenants, but it makes sense for Church history. Taking the time to do a good overview of Church history, even a segment at a time, would be helpful in developing a mental framework for better understanding the Doctrine and Covenants as well.

Remembering Church History

Having been born and raised in the Church, and having taken Church history classes in seminary, I had a basic understanding of the chronology and critical events. However, I was able to fit the sequence of events and anchor details much better into memory after visiting Church history sites, watching *Legacy*, and then reading and watching *The Work and the Glory*, and more recently *Emma Smith: My Story*.

What was also helpful to me was putting the events of Church history into chronological order by relating events to dates, as noted in chapter 5. A timeline, which included both the year and month of significant events, was a helpful reference in this regard.

Anchoring the names and events to places I had seen or could envision from movies or pictures was also helpful. Additionally, I found it of great value to have a graphic overview in mind of the Saints' migrations as supplied by the various maps of their travels. If I wanted to remember something, I could literally zoom in my mind to that particular time and place to envision the events that occurred then and there. (If you find these places hard to imagine, you might try imagining these events happening in your neighborhood or some other location you are more familiar with.)

Remembering the Doctrine and Covenants

Although I had grown up with the Doctrine and Covenants, and have known the phonetic or symbolic number system for more than twenty years, I had never systematically used it to remember the contents of the Doctrine and Covenants. However, once I set my mind to it, as described in chapter 5, I found it quite easy to do so. By taking three to five sections a day, and focusing on linking the numbers to just a few concepts in each section, I assembled most of the main themes by section in my head, in just over a month's time. You could do it faster; I was not in a rush, and this gave me time to think and link, and to consolidate the information as I went.

I also recorded my memory clues and cues. Both the process of recording and listening to them were helpful. First, I typed or drew these symbols, and the mental pictures linking them, and then I spoke these into a tape recorder. You can review these symbols and short scripts on my website at www.ARECORD4LDS.com, but symbols, pictures, or images will be more memorable for you if you come up with them, than if you were to just try and rely on mine.

These tapes were valuable; I played them on my way to work to help reinforce and maintain symbol and image integrity until I had each image firmly fixed in my memory. It is most efficient if I can visualize the same image in the same location or setting every time; the brain tends to best remember the first image that comes to mind. If I took too much time between reviews or didn't have my image down on paper or recorded, I had to reinvent some images for the next review. Taking the time to make these notes and recordings from the start was more efficient and effective in getting a strong, clear image in mind.

Some sections took much longer to learn, like section 88. And I didn't link every concept. I wanted to get a basic framework in my mind of what was in each section or where the most important doctrines are found. For this, the heading and overview for each section were of great value. In fact sometimes that was all I read to identify the main themes to link to the section number. Looking at what I had previously highlighted in each section was also helpful to identify the main or most important points for me to remember.

Sometimes the main themes are easy to visualize, like the Three Witnesses seeing the gold plates in section 17, or the sacrament prayers being given in section 20. However, in most instances it helped to select symbols to represent the themes or the most important concepts, and then link the symbols together in a picture (discussed in chapter 4) with the first content symbol representing the first idea in that section linked to the picture word (symbol) representing the section number.

When I explained this concept in chapter 4 I had not yet explained the number system. But in order to link the content or symbols discussed in section 77 with the section number, all I had to do was imagine a huge cake (77) on the ice pond. First I imagined the cake on the ice and then the beasts coming to it, followed by the elders, seals, and so forth.

As you might imagine, it is possible to confuse the content symbols with the symbol used to remember the section number. To avoid that, I made sure I had memorized and was familiar with the number symbols or picture words first. I suggest you review them periodically so that you don't confuse them with the other content. You may find it helpful to imagine these number symbols being red or some other color to help them stand out in your visualization of the section.

The further I progressed, the more time I needed to review and reinforce the material in my mind. For several days all I did was review and rehearse. Periodically, the brain just needs some time to collect itself and consolidate the information it already has.

This was a challenge for me and required a great deal of imagination and persistence. However, once accomplished, it has been a great source of satisfaction to know where I can go to find the various doctrines and teachings of this most remarkable modern scripture. Sometimes I'm stumped and still can't remember what is where. My overview did not contain all of the topics and details of each section, but these are relatively easy to add into my mental movies as needed. For additional topics or details I want to add, I can link them in some memorable way to the next closest symbol or image from the text that I've already visualized for this section.

Say if I want to remember that the method for verifying Church status when moving into a new area is in section 20, a quick review of section 20 reveals that this instruction follows the sacrament prayers, which I already have linked to a symbol for number 20 (newspaper) in my memory. To link this subject to that I imagine that after the sacrament, as the Aaronic Priesthood brethren are returning to their seats, a man who I have never seen before, who looks and is dressed like a punk rocker with a purple Mohawk, approaches the bishop with a large sheet of paper certifying that he is a member in good standing—despite his appearance.

Try Doodling as an Aid to Remembering

Especially for those who like to doodle, images or symbols they draw are much more memorable that someone else's typeset. Most of us tend to remember the things that we see much better than things we hear or read about. "A picture is worth a thousand words" is true when it comes to remembering. If you draw it yourself, it will be even more memorable, and you don't have to be an Arnold Friberg to be able to do this either. Who has not used or at least seen a drawing of circles depicting the stages of life?

Drawings like this (or much simpler) make concepts much easier to recall.

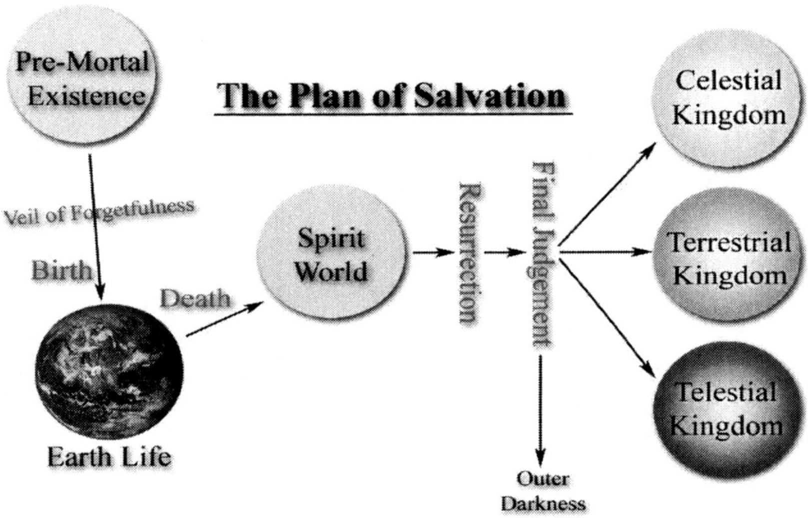

Memorizing

There are many verses in the Doctrine and Covenants you may want to memorize word for word and maybe you have already done this with many. As I've reflected back on those verses that I have memorized, there are seven practices that seem to have been most helpful for me. These are generally in line with the seven basic principles outlined in chapter 4.

1. Pay close attention to the context and the idea that is being conveyed. If we really understand the intent and meaning of a passage, it will be easier to memorize the specific words used to convey that idea or intent.

2. Connect or relate the thoughts. A friend of mine who is an artist finds it very helpful to draw symbols or pictures representing each line or key thought, which he then links together in sequence. This makes it easier for him to envision. I find it simpler to link

the ideas and images in my mind, in sequential order with the words that are used.

3. Rehearse a small section at a time until you have it down word for word. Then move on to the next phrase or idea until it is mastered, and so on. I find I need to pay most attention to the middle portion; the principles of first and last exposure seem to make it easier to remember the beginning and end portions.

4. Exaggerate pesky words. There always seems to be a few pesky words that are harder to recall. To help with these, I write out the portion I am struggling with, in long hand, EXAGGERATING the words I most often forget. Then when I deliver these out loud to myself, I emphasize those words.

5. Practice spaced repetition and rehearsal. It is best to continue rehearsing until I can do it at least once without error. Then I wait thirty seconds to a minute and rehearse it again. If I get it right the second time I stop for a while. If I get it wrong I note my error, repeat it right, and wait another thirty seconds—but not more than a minute—and try it again. Once I get it right I give it another ten to fifteen minutes and recheck to see if I've retained it. If I still remember it, it is well on its way to becoming secure in long-term memory.

6. Sleep on it. It is important, if not crucial, for my memory consolidation that I get a good night's sleep, preferably soon after my last review for the night.

7. Weekly rehearsal. Some of the scriptures I remember best are those that I learned as a young adult, when I would repeat a verse over and over week after week, for four or five weeks. That weekly rehearsal, the spaced repetition, was effective in cementing those verses into my brain.

Periodic Review

It is important to take time to periodically review all the things I want to remember, otherwise even once vivid memories can fade, especially as I grow older. One of the great things about this system is once these images have been committed to long-term memory, you can pull them up anytime, any place, for review and rehearsal. Additional reviews will likely be needed, about one month later and again several months later. One of my favorite times for review is while driving to work or returning home. All I have to do is pick a number 1 to 138, and instantly I have doctrines and teachings to review in my mind. For a more practical mental workout, I pick a topic and see what sections I can recall which talk about that topic. This of course is the most useful, for that is usually how we need to recall the information—we'll say, "Where does it talk about this?" and then, "What does it say?"

To help me with this I have prepared simple study sheets like that noted below. On the left you will see questions, in the center are the answers, and on the right are memory cues. I just fold the chart on the line so I can see only the questions, and then try to remember the answers. If I can't readily recall the answer, I take a peek to refresh it and the memory cue or clue, and then do it over from memory. I also play it like Jeopardy—look at the answer and then try to recall the question.

If my memories become too faded, I go back and play the relevant tape or tapes for the sections I want to reinforce or review.

What are parents to teach their children? Where can that be found?	D&C 68:25: repentance, faith in Christ, baptism, the gift of the Holy Ghost, prayer and to walk upright before the Lord.	Imagine a father teaching the fourth article of faith to his son while **shav**ing.
Where does it talk about the blessings of honoring the Sabbath with thanksgiving?	D&C 59:16: "Inasmuch as ye do this, the fullness of the earth is yours."	Imagine a woman in church in Jackson giving thanks and various goods fall into her **lap** from the sky.

Using Music to Enhance Memory

We know music can enhance memory but how, when, and what kind of music? Playing Mozart and other classical music to young children has been shown to be helpful in the development of their brains.[1] Learning to play a musical instrument can enhance other learning and cognitive abilities, like math for example, in elementary age children. Music can evoke memories, even in individuals with Alzheimer's disease. And tunes can be used to learn new information, such as the ABCs. What is not clear, however, is if music playing in the background can enhance other learning. For example, would it be helpful to play soft classical music or instrumental hymns in the background while studying the scriptures? Maybe so, maybe not.

Earlier studies from Bulgaria suggested that playing classical Baroque music while children were learning vocabulary words and other information could be helpful. However, in a 1983 study, students learning German with music ended up learning 50 percent less than those with no music. In another ten-week accelerated learning course at the Defense Language Institute in Monterey, California, students learning Russian accompanied by music learned 40 percent less then those who studied for fifteen weeks with more traditional methods. One explanation for this difference is that music, even classical instrumental pieces, compete for the attention of the listener—and, of course, you know the importance of paying close attention.

A more recent study of the effects of music on verbal and visual-spatial performance came to the following conclusions:

1. Those who choose music to accompany study tend to be more extraverted. Extraverts in general report that they are less bothered by noise and music.

2. People's perception of the degree to which music and noise bother them is unreliable.

3. Vocal music is more bothersome (interferes more with attention) than instrumental music.

4. Music interferes more with complex tasks than with

simple ones, and it interferes more with verbal tasks than with visual-spatial ones.[2]

So while music can be helpful and soothing for the mind, and may facilitate recalling events and ideas associated with that music, and likely will not interfere with your looking at pictures of Church history, we must conclude that it is likely not helpful in remembering things we read. It may even interfere with some learning unless you are an extrovert or really like music, in which cases you may still want to try to set some of the material you are learning to music. That can be fun, as well as making it more memorable (See *How to Remember Everything in the Book of Mormon,* chapter 9, for additional instructions in this method of learning.)

Conclusion

It's clear the Lord intends for us to both heed and remember His modern-day counsel, as contained in the Doctrine and Covenants and echoed throughout Church history. Obeying the Lord's counsel with regards to the Word of Wisdom can also help to keep our memories sharp and clear as we advance in years. Following these practices will not always be easy, but patient persistence with these proven principles, and the help of the Holy Ghost pays off. Such persistence can enable us to not only retain much more of what we read and hear, but as we seek learning, by study and also by faith, we have the potential and promise that we will gain treasures of knowledge that will not only give us an advantage in this life, but in the world to come as well. May the Lord bless you in this important endeavor.

NOTES

1. Pierce J. Howard, , *The Owner's Manual for the Brain: Everyday Applications from Mind-Brain Research* (Austin: Bard Press, 3rd Ed., 2006), 248
2. Ibid., 251

APPENDIX A

Since we tend to remember pictures in familiar places better than concepts, you may want to imagine the following in your backyard.

The First Method

Learn the rhyming symbols to represent each number, as follows:

1—sun	6—sticks	11—two suns
2—shoe	7—heaven (harp)	12—sun and shoe
3—tree	8—gate	13—sun and tree
4—door	9—dine (table)	
5—(bee) hive	10—hen	

Create a picture associating each number's symbol with a key idea for each corresponding article of faith, such as the following:

1. Sun—to remember the Godhead, imagine bright rays of sunlight shining on you, representing the light that comes from God the Father and His Son.

2. Shoe—to remember that man will be punished for his own sins, picture a man being struck with a shoe as punishment for something he did wrong.

3. Tree—to remember that through the Atonement of Christ all mankind may be saved, you can picture Jesus being hung on a cross made from a tree.

4. Door—imagine a door. On it is written the first four

principles and ordinances of the gospel, FAITH, REPENTANCE, BAPTISM, and the GIFT of the Holy Ghost.

5. Beehive—to remember that a man must be called of God by prophecy, imagine the bishop using a megaphone that looks like a beehive to call to you.

6. Sticks—to remember the sixth article talks about the Church's organization, imagine men in each priesthood office with a stick in their hands, which they use to build a church.

7. Heaven—a harp is a symbol for heaven. Imagine someone trying to play a harp with his tongue and one hand, which has a ribbon tied to each finger, representing five other spiritual gifts.

8. Gate—to remember the eighth article talks about the Bible and Book of Mormon, you might imagine a gate and hanging on it are two books tied together—the Bible and Book of Mormon.

9. Dine—imagine your dining room table and on it are the Urim and Thummim, representing all that God has revealed; a laptop computer, symbolizing what He does now reveal; and a crystal ball, showing He will yet reveal many great and important things.

10. Hen—to remember the tenth article talks about the gathering of Israel, imagine a hen trying to gather in her chicks under her wings.

11. Two suns—imagine kneeling and worshipping God, with a ray of light shining on you. Next to you is a person of another faith on his knees worshipping with a ray of light shining on him too.

12. Sun and shoe—to remember that the twelfth article talks about being subject to kings, presidents, and rulers, imagine a ray of light shining on a king pounding a podium with a shoe as he prepares to tell his people what to do.

13. Sun and tree—imagine a ray of light carving or writing these beliefs on the trunk of a tree, "honest, true, chaste, benevolent, virtuous, doing good, Paul."

Second Method

The second method focuses on the number on the numbered

article to remember what it is about. For the first Article of Faith, for example, it emphasizes *one.*

1. We believe in only one God the Eternal Father, and one Godhead.

2. We believe man will be punished for his own sins and not for what a second person has done. Adam and Eve were the first two people on earth to sin.

3. This talks about the requirements for salvation: 1) the Atonement and then obedience, 2) the laws, and 3) the ordinances of the gospel. Also the cross, the symbol of the Atonement has three points or ends.

4. Talks about the first four principles of the gospel.

5. Talks about being called of God by prophecy and by the laying on of hands (a hand has five fingers) by one in authority. Authority comes after the first four basic principles of the gospel.

6. This talks about six of the same organizational callings that existed in the Primitive Church. After men are given the authority (see the fifth Article) they can act in these various offices.

7. This talks about seven gifts—T-P-R-V-H-I-S are the first letters of each. Can you make up a word or sentence from these letters? How about "Tongues Prophesy about Revelations, Visions, Healings, and the Interpretation of tongues and So forth." These gifts are given to men following the six callings noted above.

8. If the Bible and Book of Mormon were written on scrolls stacked on top of each other, looking at them from the ends they would look like an 8.

9. We believe in three things, in three different time zones: all that God has revealed, all that He does now reveal, and all that He will yet reveal many great and important things (these are three adjectives used to describe what God reveals; 3 x 3 = 9).

10. We believe in the gathering of the ten tribes.

11. The eleven is made up of two ones—one for us and one for others. We claim the privilege for each of us of worshipping God according to the dictates of our own conscience.

12. We believe in being subject to rulers, among others, and a ruler has twelve inches.

13. There are at least thirteen beliefs and virtues mentioned here, plus Paul who could be called the thirteenth apostle of Jesus.

Practice these over and over, until you can easily recall and recite each out of order.

APPENDIX B

TIMELINE OF SOME EVENTS IN CHURCH HISTORY

1805	Dec. 23	Joseph Smith Jr. born in Sharon, Vermont
1820	Spring	Joseph Smith visited by the Father and the Son, in a grove near the Smith home in Manchester, New York
1823		**Section 2**
	Sept. 21	Moroni appears to Joseph Smith, Manchester, New York. Joseph was 17
1827		
	Sept. 22	Joseph Smith obtains the gold plates of the Book of Mormon at Palmyra, New York
1828		**Section 3, 10**
		Loss of the 116 manuscript pages of the Book of Mormon at Palmyra, New York

1829	**Section 4, 5, 6, 7, 8, 9, 11, 12, 13, 14, 15, 16, 17, 18**
May 15	John the Baptist restores the Aaronic Priesthood at Harmony, Pennsylvania
June	Peter, James, and John restore the Melchizedek Priesthood between Colesville, New York, and Harmony, Pennsylvania
June	Gold plates shown to three and eight witnesses, Fayette, New York
June 11	Copyright for the Book of Mormon obtained

1830	**Sections 19 thru 37**
March	Book of Mormon published, Palmyra, New York
Apr. 6	Church organized at Fayette, New York
Jun. 9	First conference of the church held, Fayette, New York
June	First missionary, Samuel H. Smith, sent out
July	Emma Smith called to make a selection of hymns, Harmony, Pennsylvania
Oct	Lamanite missionaries leave New York

1831	**Sections 1, 38 thru 72, 133**
February	Joseph Smith moves to Kirtland, Ohio
Feb. 4	Edward Partridge called as first bishop, Kirtland, Ohio
May	Missionaries sent to the Shakers
June	First ordinations of High Priests were made (conference June 3rd to 6th)
July	Location of the city of Zion revealed

Aug. 2	Land of Zion dedicated in Kaw Township, Missouri
Aug. 3	Temple site in Independence, Missouri, dedicated

1832	**Sections 73 thru 88**
Jan. 25	Joseph Smith sustained as President of High Priesthood at Amherst, Ohio
Mar. 24	Joseph Smith and Sidney Rigdon mobbed at Hiram, Ohio
June	First Periodical of the Church, Evening and Morning Star, published at Independence, Missouri
December	School of the prophets established at Kirtland, Ohio

---

1833	**Sections 89 thru 101**
Feb	Word of Wisdom
Mar 18	First Presidency organized at Kirtland, Ohio
Jul 2	Joseph Smith "finished" translation of the Bible, Kirtland, Ohio
Jul 23	Cornerstones of Kirtland Temple laid
November	Saints driven out of Jackson County, Missouri
Dec 18	First Patriarch to the Church called, Joseph Smith Sr. at Kirtland, Ohio

---

1834	**Sections 102 thru 106**
	United Order

1835	**Sections 107, 108, 134** Three witnesses choose the first Twelve Apostles of this dispensation
1836	**Sections 109, 110, 111, and 137** Kirtland Temple dedicated, ordinances of endowment revealed
1837	**Section 112**
1838	**Sections 113 thru 120** Haun's Mill Massacre Tithing; winter of 1838–39, Saints moved to Illinois
1839	**Sections 121, 122, 123** Joseph imprisoned in Liberty Jail
1840	**None**
1841	**Sections 124, 125, 126**
1842	**Sections 127, 128** Baptism for the dead, Relief Society organized
1843	**Sections 129 thru 132** Everlasting covenant of marriage, plural marriage
1844	**Section 135** Joseph Smith and Hyrum killed in Carthage
1845	**None**
1846	**None**
1847	Section 136
1918	**Section 138**

REFERENCES

Alzheimer's Association, "Maintain Your Brain, How to Live a Brain Healthy Lifestyle," *Participants Workbook*, 2006, and Alzheimer's Disease, "Risk Factors." www.alz.org/alzheimers_disease_causes_risk_factors.asp#riskfactors.

Alzheimer's Association, *2008 Alzheimer's Disease Facts and Figures*, 34. Accessed from www.alz.org.

BYU Newsnet: News from the Y. "Sleep Crucial to Grades," Kristen Radford. 13 Mar 2007. http://newsnet.byu.edu/story.cfm/63515.

Benson, Ezra Taft. "In His Steps." *1979 Devotional Speeches of the Year*, Provo, Utah: BYU, 1980, 62.

———. "Do Not Despair," *Ensign*, Nov. 1974, 65.

Documented History of the Church Vol. 6, 314.

Grant, William B. "Dietary Links to Alzheimer's Disease." *Alzheimer's Disease Review* 2, 1997, 42–55.

Johnson, Carla K. "Kids Fear 2 Parents With Alzheimer's," ABC News, 10 March 2008. http://abcnews.go.com/Health/MindMoodNews/wireStory?id=4423128.

Joyal, Steven V. *What Your Doctor May Not Tell You About Diabetes.* FL: Life Extension Publications, 2008.

Kivipelto, Miia et al. "Body Mass Index, clustering, of vascular risk factors, and the risk of dementia: A longitudinal, population-based study." *Neurobiology of Aging* July 2004, Vol. 25 S2, p. S311.

Linus Pauling Institute, Oregon State University. "Micronutrients Information Center." http://lpi.oregonstate.edu/infocenter/vitamins/vitaminB12/b12refs.html#ref16.

Little, Andrew. "Spiritually fit but not physically fit." Scroll Online: Brigham Young University—Idaho. 7 June 2006, www.byui.edu/Scroll/archive/20060606/news3.html.

Maas, J. B. *Power Sleep*, New York: Villard Books, 1998.

"Major Trends in U.S. Food Supply, 1909–99," *Food Review*, Vol. 23, Iss. 1. Available at www.ers.usda.gov/publications/foodreview/jan2000/frjan2000b.pdf.

Maquet, P. et al. "Experience-dependent changes in cerebral activation during human REM sleep," *Nature Neuroscience*, 3:831–836, 2000. Online: www.nature.com/neuro/journal/v3/n8/abs/nn0800_831.html.

Medical News Today. "Education—The Best Pill Of All For Preventing Alzheimer's." www.medicalnewstoday.com/medicalnews.php?newsid=59612.

Merrill, A. Roger. "Receiving by the Spirit," *Ensign*, Nov. 2006, 92–94.

Mortimer JA et al. "Very early detection of Alzheimer neuropathology and the role of brain reserve in modifying its clinical expression." *Journal of Geriatric Psychiatry and Neurology*, 18(4):218–223, 2005.

Nedley, Neil. *Depression Recovery Program*, Ardmore, OK: Nedley Publishing, 2006.

Pasinetti, Giulio. "Animal study indicates grape seed extract may reduce cognitive decline associated with Alzheimer's disease." SfN News Releases, 17 June 2008. www.sfn.org/?pagename=news_061708b.

Perlmutter, David. *The Better Brain Book*. New York: Berkley Publishing, 2004.

Scarmeas, Nicholas et al. "Mediterranean Diet, Alzheimer's Disease, and Vascular Mediation." *Archives of Neurology*, 2006; 63:1709–1717.

Seshadri S. et al. "Plasma homocysteine as a risk factor for dementia and Alzheimer's disease." *New England Journal of Medicine* 2002; 346(7):476–483.

Society for Neuroscience, Brain Briefings. SfN, "Sleeping and Learning," April 2003. http://www.sfn.org/index.cfm?pagename=brainBriefings_sleepAndLearning.

Smith, Joseph. *History of The Church of Jesus Christ of Latter-day Saints*, edited by B. H. Roberts. 2d ed. rev. 7 vols. Salt Lake City: The Church of Jesus Christ of Latter-day Saints, 1932–51.

Star Sleeper, "NHLBI'S Children and Sleep Campaign Promotes Adequate Sleep for the New School Year." July 16, 2001. www.nhlbi.nih.gov/new/press/01-02-07.htm

Teachings of the Presidents of the Church: Wilford Woodruff. Salt Lake City: The Church of Jesus Christ of Latter-day Saints, 2004.

University of Kentucky Chandler Medical Center. "Scientific." http://www.mc.uky.edu/nunnet/scientific.htm.

Watson, Elden J. *The Manuscript History of Brigham Young 1846–1847*. Salt lake City, UT: Elden J. Watson, 1971.

Zandi, Peter P. et al. "Reduced Risk of Alzheimer's Disease in Users of Antioxidant Vitamin Supplements: The Cache County Study." *Archives of Neurology* 2004; 61:82–88.

ABOUT THE AUTHOR

David R. Larsen was born and raised on a family farm in Logan, Utah. He attended Utah State University on a track scholarship and majored in education, after which he served a mission to Argentina, spent three years in the Army, and married Maureen Kulinicz of Coventry, England, in Switzerland. They have two children and five grandchildren.

He returned to the States to complete his bachelor of arts degree at the University of Utah. He later received an MS in family and human development from Utah State University and an equivalency in counseling psychology from Brigham Young University. For seven years David served as a chaplain in the Navy and Marine Corps. He has taught numerous classes related to family, organizational, and human development in England, Germany, Norway, and the United States. He is the former director of the Organizational Health Center at Hill Air Force Base and and currently manages a grant for the Alzheimer's Association where he also trains trainers for the Maintain Your Brain™ program. He also teaches classes on memory enhancement for Weber State University and is on the board of the Utah chapter of the International Association for Near-Death Studies.

0 26575 52392 8